my revision notes

Cambridge Technicals Level 3

IT

Mo Everett

HODDER
EDUCATION
AN HACHETTE UK COMPANY

The Publishers would like to thank the following for permission to reproduce copyright material.

Fig.1.1 © Swapan/stock.adobe.com; Fig.1.2 © Destina/stock.adobe.com; Fig.1.3 © creative soul/stock.adobe.com; Fig.1.5 © David Acosta Allely – Fotolia; Fig.1.6 © Stuart Fox/Gallo Images/Getty Images; Fig.1.7 © bernardbodo/stock.adobe.com; Fig.2.1 © Asta Plechaviciute/stock.adobe.com; Fig.2.2 © StudioLaMagica/stock.adobe.com; Fig.2.3 © Anna Delaw/Alamy Stock Photo; Fig.2.5 © Cultura Creative/Alamy Stock Photo; Fig.3.2 © jcdaddi – Fotolia; Fig.3.3 © SmartWater Technology Limited; Fig.3.4 © Bavorndej/stock.adobe.com.

Although every effort has been made to ensure that website addresses are correct at time of going to press, Hodder Education cannot be held responsible for the content of any website mentioned in this book. It is sometimes possible to find a relocated web page by typing in the address of the home page for a website in the URL window of your browser.

Hachette UK's policy is to use papers that are natural, renewable and recyclable products and made from wood grown in sustainable forests. The logging and manufacturing processes are expected to conform to the environmental regulations of the country of origin.

Orders: please contact Hachette UK Distribution, Hely Hutchinson Centre, Milton Road, Didcot, Oxfordshire, OX11 7HH. Telephone: +44 (0)1235 827827. Email education@hachette.co.uk Lines are open from 9 a.m. to 5 p.m., Monday to Friday.
You can also order through our website:www.hoddereducation.com

ISBN: 978-1-5104-4231-3

© Mo Everett 2018

First published in 2018 by
Hodder Education,
An Hachette UK Company
Carmelite House
50 Victoria Embankment
London EC4Y 0DZ
www.hoddereducation.co.uk

Impression number   10   9   8   7   6

Year   2023

Cover photo © Maksym Yemelyanov – stock.adobe.com

Typeset in India.

Printed and bound by CPI Group (UK) Ltd, Croydon, CR0 4YY

A catalogue record for this title is available from the British Library.

MIX
Paper from
responsible sources
FSC™ C104740

Get the most from this book

Everyone has a different approach to how they revise and, in particular, what works for them. Whatever method you use, it is always important that you review your work, learn it and then put your knowledge and understanding to the test.

These revision notes will guide you through the examinable units, helping you to ensure that you have covered all of the teaching content in sufficient depth. As IT is always changing, there are some sections where you may be asked to complete the information for yourself based on the notes from the lessons you have attended with your teachers.

After the sections on the content of the units, you will find a section on exam techniques. It is important that you study this section also: it will not matter how much you have learnt if you cannot apply that knowledge and understanding in an exam situation. After this, there is a glossary of terms that will help you refer to some of the technical words that you will come across.

Your teachers will provide you with access to past exam papers so that you can test your exam techniques and use of knowledge and understanding under exam conditions.

Tick to track your progress

Use the revision planner to plan your revision unit by unit and learning outcome by learning outcome, as well as the exam techniques that you have learnt. Tick each box when you have:
- revised and understood the assessment criteria
- revised and understood the different exam techniques
- successfully tested yourself using past papers.

Remember

This is your revision guide, so it is important that you use it effectively to meet your individual needs. You may find it useful to add additional notes as you work through the various topics.

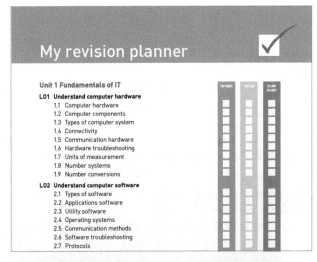

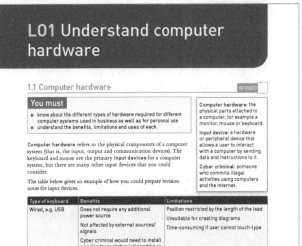

Features to help you succeed

The revision guide is broken down unit by unit, so you have:

- Unit 1 Fundamentals of IT
- Unit 2 Global information
- Unit 3 Cyber security

Within each unit you will see the learning outcome title and the relevant topic for each learning outcome.

You must

This emphasises what you need to know and understand, as well as what you must be able to do.

Now test yourself

These short, knowledge-based questions provide the first step in testing your learning.

Definitions and key words

Clear, concise definitions of essential key terms are provided where they first appear.

Revision activities

There are revision activities throughout the book. These include completing tables with information you have learnt in class, and carrying out research, for example to recommend an IT system to a particular business.

Exam techniques

Guidance on how to use the pre-released case studies for Units 2 and 3 effectively is given, as well as how to answer the questions in the context of the case studies. There is also guidance on how to answer questions that include the words 'explain', 'justify', 'analyse' and 'evaluate', as well as level of response questions.

Preparation for revision

Remember: the main reason why people fail exams is a lack of study beforehand.

- There is quality and there is quantity – neither is a substitute for the other.
- You will need to do a lot of reading about the subject.
- Make notes as you study. If you cannot think of anything to write down from a page, you have not read it sufficiently or carefully enough.
- Practise, practise, practise. Do as many past exam papers as you can. There are only so many questions an examiner can ask.
- Play to your strengths and work on your weaknesses. During an exam, you will answer questions that you know the best and find the easiest; this is called 'playing to your strengths'. When revising, do the complete opposite and work on the areas where you are weaker; this is called 'working on your weaknesses'.

Revision techniques

- Spread out your revision – do not leave it until the last minute.
- Don't be afraid to fail. Practising with past exam papers will help you to improve and, by the time the exam day arrives, you will be more confident.
- Try to recreate exam conditions while you revise: time yourself; hone your skills for reading and answering questions under timed conditions.
- Do not just read through your notes and try to memorise them. Make further notes from them to reinforce your understanding.

My revision planner

Unit 1 Fundamentals of IT

	REVISED	TESTED	EXAM READY

LO1 Understand computer hardware
- 1.1 Computer hardware
- 1.2 Computer components
- 1.3 Types of computer system
- 1.4 Connectivity
- 1.5 Communication hardware
- 1.6 Hardware troubleshooting
- 1.7 Units of measurement
- 1.8 Number systems
- 1.9 Number conversions

LO2 Understand computer software
- 2.1 Types of software
- 2.2 Applications software
- 2.3 Utility software
- 2.4 Operating systems
- 2.5 Communication methods
- 2.6 Software troubleshooting
- 2.7 Protocols

LO3 Understand business IT systems
- 3.1 Types of servers
- 3.2 Virtualisation
- 3.3 Networking characteristics
- 3.4 Connectivity methods
- 3.5 Business systems

LO4 Understand employability and communication skills used in an IT environment
- 4.1 Communication skills
- 4.2 Communication technology
- 4.3 Personal attributes
- 4.4 Ready for work
- 4.5 Job roles
- 4.6 Professional bodies
- 4.7 Industry certification

LO5 Understand ethical and operational issues and threats to computer systems
- 5.1 Ethical issues

REVISED   TESTED   EXAM READY

REVISED   TESTED   EXAM READY

LO1 Understand computer hardware

1.1 Computer hardware

> ### You must
>
> - know about the different types of hardware required for different computer systems used in business as well as for personal use
> - understand the benefits, limitations and uses of each.

Computer hardware refers to the physical components of a computer system (that is, the input, output and communication devices). The keyboard and mouse are the primary **input devices** for a computer system, but there are many other input devices that you could consider.

The table below gives an example of how you could prepare revision notes for input devices.

> **Computer hardware**: the physical parts attached to a computer, for example a monitor, mouse or keyboard.
>
> **Input device**: a hardware or peripheral device that allows a user to interact with a computer by sending data and instructions to it.
>
> **Cyber criminal**: someone who commits illegal activities using computers and the internet.

Type of keyboard	Benefits	Limitations
Wired, e.g. USB	Does not require any additional power source Not affected by external sources/signals Cyber criminal would need to install a keylogger to gather information on what is being typed in	Position restricted by the length of the lead Unsuitable for creating diagrams Time-consuming if user cannot touch-type
Wireless, e.g. Bluetooth	Can be placed at any convenient location on the desk Reduces workspace clutter	Requires powering by batteries Can be affected by other nearby wi-fi signals **Cyber criminals** can intercept signals as most wireless keyboards are unencrypted and unsecured Unsuitable for creating diagrams Time-consuming if user cannot touch-type
Integrated, e.g. laptops (although an external keyboard can be attached)	Smaller than a standard keyboard More mobile	Keys closer together can mean more typing errors Can have a lack of control keys or keypad
On screen, e.g. smartphones, tablets, touchscreen monitors (on-screen keyboards)	More mobile	Small, which can affect typing speed and accuracy Fingerprints can cause functionality issues Smaller screen restricts readability

A business has received numerous requests from its employees to have wireless keyboards instead of wired ones. The business has asked for your advice on whether it is something they should consider doing.

- Identify which keyboard you would recommend.
- **Explain** why the keyboard you have recommended would be more appropriate for the employees.

Examples of other input devices include:

- barcode readers
- biometrics
- digital cameras
- gamepads, joysticks
- light pens
- magnetic strip readers
- microphones
- mouse
- scanners
- stylus
- webcam
- graphics tablet.

Research some of the other input devices commonly used in business and for personal use. Make a note of the uses, benefits and limitations for each one.

Explain: leads on from a description to include the purpose or reasons.

Output device: a peripheral that receives data and instructions from a computer system to display, project or physically reproduce data that has been processed or stored.

Resolution: the number of horizontal and vertical pixels on a monitor; the higher the number of pixels, the higher the resolution. More screen image can be displayed without scrolling. The image is sharper, but the icons and text will look smaller.

Output devices can come in many formats, for example:

- hard copy (printed on paper, card, etc.)
- on screen
- audio
- video.

The table below is an example of how you could prepare revision notes for output devices.

Type of monitor	Benefits	Limitations
CRT (cathode ray tube); rarely used, as old technology		Heavy, bulky and costly to replace
LCD (liquid crystal display)	Compact size, which makes them lightweight Does not consume as much electricity as a CRT monitor Can run off batteries, so ideal for laptops Transmitted images are not geometrically distorted and have little flicker	Relatively high cost Image quality not consistent if viewed from different angles **Resolution** of monitor is not always constant Alterations to resolution can result in reduced performance
LED (light-emitting diodes)	Uses less power than CRT or LCD monitors, therefore more environmentally friendly Displayed images have higher contrast Less negative impact on the environment when disposed of More durable than CRT or LCD monitors Features a very thin design Does not produce a lot of heat when running	More expensive

Type of monitor	Benefits	Limitations
Touchscreen	Increased desk space (depending on the use; you do not have to attach a keyboard or mouse) Easier to use for novice computer users Increased speed compared to using a keyboard or mouse to move and select objects Easier to clean than a regular monitor as it is made out of glass or something similar	Users must sit closer to the screen in order to touch it Depending on the size of the screen and the size of the icons/text, it may be difficult to touch small objects on the screen Displays get dirty because of the constant touching with fingers

Things to consider when selecting a monitor:
- where the monitor is to be used (for example desktop, laptop)
- what type of work will be carried out on it (for example, graphic designers tend to access multiple windows and use high-resolution screens)
- whether there is a budget restriction with respect to cost
- what features are required (for example does it have a swivel base; does it have an adjustable height?)
- size: this links in with where it is to be used and the purpose
- second monitor: again this links to purpose; would the user benefit from dual displays?

Revision activity

A web development business is upgrading its computer system and is looking for advice on which monitors to purchase for the following departments:
- finance
- web and graphic design
- administration.

Recommend monitors for each of the departments and justify the recommendations you have made.

Examples of other output devices include:
- printers
- plotters
- headphones
- speakers
- projectors.

Revision activity

Research some of the other output devices commonly used in business and for personal use. Make a note of the uses, benefits and limitations of each one. Put your notes in a table similar to the one created for monitors above.

Remember

Some devices are known as input/output (I/O) devices, for example:
- headphones with a microphone
- touchscreen monitors.

Communication device: a hardware device that transmits data from one machine to another using analogue or digital signals.

It is important to consider how input and output devices can be used by business as well as from a personal point of view.

The following table considered the features, uses and purpose of a range of **communication devices**.

Type of communication device	Features, uses and purpose
Smartphone	Small computer that also functions as a telephone. Features can include: ● digital voice service ● internet access ● email and text messaging ● MP3 player ● digital camera/video recorder ● a wide range of computer applications for business
Laptop	Mobile computer Similar functionality to a PC Allows internet access for instant messaging, email and video conferencing
Bluetooth device	Enables devices to communicate with each other using radio frequency (RF) technology; for example: ● headphones ● keyboard and mouse ● speaker ● smartwatch or health monitor ● car (for hands-free calls) ● lock (to remotely lock and unlock a door)
Infrared (IR) device	Allows for the transference of data wirelessly, for example: ● remote control ● keyboard and mouse
Router	Allows multiple computers to join the same network (this can be through the ethernet ports or wirelessly)
Modem	Connects to the internet service provider (ISP) either through cable, digital subscriber line (DSL) or fibre-optic internet service. **Cable modems** have a coaxial connection (similar to a TV or cable box); **DSL modems** have a RJ-11 connection (same as a telephone connector), which connects to a telephone socket in the wall. Because the final part of the fibre-optic signal is sent over a copper coaxial cable, a modem is still required
Hybrid	A modem and router combined into a single device; usually offered by ISPs to make the set-up process easier
Network interface card (NIC)	An expansion card that enables a computer to connect to a network using an ethernet cable (most computers have a network interface built into the **motherboard**)
Wi-fi adapter	Integrated (built-in) as standard on new computers USB network adapters plug into a standard USB port

Modem (cable): MOdulator/DEModulator; a hardware device that enables a computer to send and receive information over telephone lines by converting digital data into an analogue signal.

Modem (DSL): a hardware device that allows a computer to communicate with an ISP over a DSL connection. A traditional phone line (RJ-11) connects to the back of the DSL modem and the Cat5 (ethernet) cable connects the modem to a router or computer.

Motherboard: a printed circuit board connecting all of the peripherals and components of a computer enabling them to communicate. It regulates the power received by the hard drive, graphics card, central processing unit (CPU) and system memory from the power supply.

Revision activity

Research the communication devices given in the table above. Create a table similar to the one below to record the benefits and limitations of each. You should also think about different businesses and how they may use these devices, as well as personal use.

Communication device	Benefits	Limitations	Type of business	How it would be used	Personal use
Smartphone					
Laptop					
Bluetooth device					
Infrared (IR) device					
Router					
Modem					
Hybrid					
Network interface card (NIC)					
Wi-fi adapter					

Now test yourself

TESTED ☐

1   Explain one advantage and one disadvantage of an integrated keyboard.
2   A supermarket asks customers to answer a short online questionnaire before leaving the shop. The customers stand in front of a screen which has a series of yes/no questions to answer. Which type of input device would be the most appropriate for customers to use? Justify your answer.
3   What type of hardware device is a headphone with a microphone attached?
4   Explain what a network interface card (NIC) is.

1.2 Computer components

You must

- know about the different component parts of a computer system and their **characteristics**
- understand the purpose of each component.

Characteristic: a feature or quality of something that helps to identify it.

Computer components: the internal elements of a computer system enabling it to run, for example processor, storage, power supply.

Computer components are the physical parts of a computer system.

Component	Characteristics	Purpose
Processor	Make and model (e.g. although they have similar features and performance, you cannot install an AMD processor in an Intel-compatible motherboard and vice versa)	
	Socket type (e.g. not interchangeable between AMD and Intel processors)	
	Clock speed (determines the performance; the more instructions that can be completed per second, the faster the data can be processed)	
	Host-bus speed/front-side bus speed (the data transfer rate between the processor and the chipset)	
	Cache memory (stores frequently used data and instructions; the more cache memory, the faster the access to data)	
	Size (smaller processors use a lower voltage, consume less power and produce less heat)	
	Special features (e.g. SSE3, or Streaming Single-Instruction-Multiple Data (SIMD) Extension 3; 64-bit support; protected execution; power reduction technology, dual-core support)	
Motherboard	Form factor (size, shape, position of mounting holes, power supply connector type, port types and locations)	
	Processor socket and chipset (depends on the processor to be installed)	
	Slots (types and quantity to accommodate RAM, graphics cards etc.)	
	Connectors	
	Special features (e.g. allow overclocking)	
Storage	**Hard drive:** ● electro-mechanical device ● uses one or more rotating discs ● relies on magnetic storage ● slower access speeds than SSDs ● can be internal (within the casing of the PC) or external (connected by a cable to the PC, which makes it removable) **Solid state:** ● no moving parts, so more robust than hard drives ● data stored electronically instead of magnetically ● most SSDs use flash memory ● faster access speeds than hard disk drives ● can be internal or external, the same as hard disk drives ● external SSDs are more portable due to their smaller size ● limited read/write cycles **Flash drive:** ● lightweight ● micro-portable	

Cloud:
- manageability (manage a system with minimal resources)
- access method (the protocol through which cloud storage is accessed)
- performance (measured in bandwidth and latency)
- multi-tenancy (accessible to multiple users)
- scalability (can scale up or down depending on storage needs)
- data availability (ability for the cloud storage provider to provide the data back to the user upon request)
- control (customer's ability to control and manage how the data is stored and the costs associated with the importance of the data)
- storage efficiency (the more data stored, the greater the efficiency)
- cost (the ability to reduce costs using the cloud, e.g. the cost of purchasing storage, powering storage, repairing/replacing storage when a drive fails and managing the storage)

SAS (serial-attached SCSI):
- faster and more reliable than SATA drives
- SAS drives tend to be used for enterprise computing, where high speed and high availability are critical
- SAS drives have a lower storage capacity than SATA drives
- cables up to 10 metres in length
- power and data provided through the same cable

SATA (serial advanced technology attachment):
- tends to be used for desktops, data storage and backups
- SATA cables limited to 1 metre in length
- data and power cables are separate

SCSI (small computer system interface):
- uses a single cable
- has its own unique controller
- can work with different computer types
- fast
- more expensive
- hard to configure as each device has its own unique identification

Ports

USB (universal serial bus):
- USB-compliant devices receive power from a USB port
- used to connect a wide variety of external devices
- host-based (devices must be connected to a computer to communicate)

Firewire:
- used for devices working with higher levels of data, e.g. DVD players, digital audio equipment
- more expensive than USB
- peer-to-peer (two 'firewire' devices can communicate with each other without going through the computer)
- firewire devices can be powered or unpowered
- supports isochronous devices (where data transfers continuously and at a steady rate closely timed with the receipt and display of the image data)

SATA (see above)

	Network (e.g. ethernet port): ● used to connect wired network hardware ● uses an RJ-45 connector **Fibre channel:** ● suited for connecting computer services to shared storage devices, interconnecting storage controllers and drives ● faster than SCSI ● more flexible (devices can be longer distances apart if optical fibre is used) ● can work using coaxial cable and telephone twisted pair ● offers point-to-point, switched and loop interfaces	
Memory	**RAM (Random Access Memory):** ● fast ● volatile (if a computer loses power, all data in the RAM is lost) ● stores the operating system, applications, and graphical user interface (GUI) **ROM (Read Only Memory):** ● cannot be changed by a program or a user ● is not volatile (retains its memory even after computer is switched off) ● stores the start-up instructions of the computer **Cache (high-speed memory in the CPU):** ● speeds up access to data and instructions stored in RAM ● holds frequently requested data and instructions so that they are available to the CPU when required ● two types: internal cache (within the processor) and external cache (on the motherboard)	
Expansion cards including: ● interface cards, e.g. firewire, IDE, SCSI, USB, fibre channel, storage controller ● modem ● network card ● sound card ● video card		Expansion cards are circuit boards that provide additional facilities or memory. Interfaces such as SAS, SATA and SCSI are used for transferring data to and from hard drives (often used to describe types of hard drive)

Now test yourself

TESTED ☐

1 Describe **two** characteristics of cloud storage.
2 What is the purpose of cache?
3 An organisation needs to use storage drives where high speed and high availability of data are critical.
   Which type of drive would you recommend? Justify your choice of drive.
4 Describe the difference between ROM and RAM.
5 A business is trying to decide which storage medium to use to store the large amounts of data that they use. The business has offices in various locations across the UK and Europe. Recommend a storage medium and justify why this storage medium would meet their requirements.

Processor: carries out the instructions of a computer program; it performs the mathematical, logical and input/output operations of a computer system.

Describe: to write about something giving its characteristics and qualities.

1.3 Types of computer system

You must

- know about the different types of computer system
- understand where and how they are used
- understand the benefits and limitation of each type of system
- be able to justify the selection of a computer system in a given context.

Types of computer systems include:

- **Desktop/server** – there are many types of server, for example proxy, network, file, virtual server.
- **Tablet/hybrid** – a hybrid is a tablet that is also a laptop and has a removable keyboard.
- **Smartphone** – contains an integrated computer.
- **Embedded system/Internet of Things** – a combination of computer hardware and software designed for a specific function or functions within a larger system.
- **Mainframe** – a high-performance computer used for large-scale computer purposes.
- **Quantum** – still in research phase but has the potential to solve complex problems beyond the capacity of the standard computer by utilising the principles of quantum physics.

Internet of Things: futuristic concept in which ordinary physical objects will be connected to the internet and be able to identify themselves to other devices.

Computer type	Uses	Benefits	Limitations
Tablet	Second screen for a PC	Portability	Prone to damage
	Remote control	Long battery life	Screen size smaller than a laptop
	Ereader	Less weight than a laptop	High cost
	Portable media and gaming centre	Smaller in size	Does not come with optical drives
	Viewer for graphics, video, presentations	Flexible screen (portrait or landscape)	Lower type and speed of input process
	Taking notes	Handwriting recognition	Fingerprints and dirt on touchscreens reduce visibility and functionality
		Can be used as a GPS device	Touchscreen typing is not as quick (or accurate) as using a larger, separate keyboard
		Offers similar functionality to a standard computer	

Revision activity

For each of the computer types above, create a table to identify the uses, benefits and limitations. An example is given above.

Now test yourself

TESTED

1. Identify a household appliance that would include an embedded system.
2. Describe **two** limitations of using a tablet.
3. Which type of computer system uses qubits?
4. Describe two reasons why an organisation would use a mainframe computer system.
5. Discuss the benefits to a remote worker of using a smartphone.

Discuss: talk about a topic.

1.4 Connectivity

REVISED

You must

- know the different connectivity methods
- know the characteristics of each connectivity method
- understand the purpose of each connectivity method
- be able to justify different connectivity methods for a given context.

Characteristics of **copper cables**:
- limited bandwidth
- less expensive when used to connect network devices
- already available in rural areas.

Characteristics of **fibre cables**:
- increased bandwidth
- long-distance capabilities
- can provide phone and internet service on same fibre
- enhanced performance reliability
- faster transmission rates than copper
- less attenuation than copper (that is, less signal loss over distance)
- impervious to electromagnetic interference
- not a fire hazard as they do not conduct electricity
- do not break easily
- expensive.

Figure 1.1 Copper cable

Characteristics of **wireless technologies**:
- uses radio waves
- infrastructure does not yet cover all remote areas
- signals degrade with distance.

Revision activity

Complete the table below for each of the connectivity methods to include their purpose and when and how they are used.

Connectivity method	Purpose	Reason for use
Copper cables		
Fibre cables		
Wireless technologies		

Figure 1.2 Fibre cable

Now test yourself

TESTED

1. Explain two advantages of using fibre-optic cabling over copper cabling.
2. Microwave is a 'line-of-sight' technology. Explain what this means.
3. GSM supports multiple frequencies. True or false?
4. Give **two** examples of the use of infrared wireless technology within the home.

1.5 Communication hardware

You must

- know about the different communication hardware devices
- know the characteristics of different communication hardware
- understand the purpose of different communication hardware
- understand the use of different communication hardware.

Communication hardware	Characteristics	Purpose
Hub	Three basic types: passive, active and intelligent **Passive**: - does not amplify the electrical signal of incoming packets before broadcasting them out to the network - can be referred to as a concentrator **Active**: - amplifies the electrical signal of incoming packets (same as a repeater) - can be referred to as a multiport repeater **Intelligent**: - stackable - includes remote management capabilities via SNMP (Simple Network Management Protocol) and virtual LAN (VLAN) support Hubs are slower as they cannot send and receive information at the same time Hubs broadcasts to every port and place a lot of traffic on the network, leading to poor network response times	Join multiple computers or other network devices together to form a single network segment Used to connect segments of a LAN Useful for replacing a broken network switch temporarily or when performance is not a critical factor on the network Handles a data type known as frames (frames carry the data); when a frame is received, it is amplified and then transmitted on to the port of the destination PC
Switch	Learns where particular addresses are Networks are faster Network traffic goes where it needs to rather than to every port Uses a table of MAC addresses to determine the port to which the data is to be sent Connects LAN segments Can operate multiple media, e.g. coaxial cable, UTP and fibre Can work different technologies with different speeds Provides routing capabilities Provides an expanded bandwidth	Does the same as a hub but more efficiently Channels incoming data from multiple input ports to the specific output port

Communication hardware	Characteristics	Purpose
Router	Multiport devices with high-speed **backbones** Support filtering and **encapsulation** Self-learning (same as bridges) Less susceptible to catastrophic failure	Used to connect similar and dissimilar LANs Routes traffic by considering the network as a whole Constantly monitors the condition of the network to adapt to changes Joins a home or business network (LAN) to the internet (WAN)
Modem	Different modems have different bps rates (speed at which they transmit and receive data) Connected using RS-232 connectors Can come as an expansion board (called internal modems) Support a switch to change between voice and data modes Can include auto-answer and will receive calls in the absence of the user Some modems perform data compression and can send data faster, but the receiving modem must support the same data compression technique Some modems come with flash memory Most modems are fax modems	Converts digital signals generated by the computer to analogue signals that can be transmitted over a telephone, cable or satellite line; transforms incoming analogue signals into their digital equivalents
Wireless access point	Can be known as a 'hotspot' Feature radio transmitters and antennae enabling connectivity between devices and the internet or network	A hardware device or configured node on a LAN that allows wireless-capable devices and wired networks to connect through a wireless standard, including wi-fi and Bluetooth Used in office environments, allowing employees to work anywhere in the office and remain connected to a network Can provide wireless internet in public places such as coffee shops, airports and train stations
Combined/hybrid devices	A device that combines the functionality of a number of communication hardware devices, e.g. combining the functionality of a modem, router, switch and WAP	Provides a common hybrid access point, e.g. hybrid router Broadcasts a wi-fi signal as well as containing ethernet ports for connecting wired devices; it would also have a port for connecting to a cable or DSL modem via an ethernet cable Allows for the mobility and flexibility of a wireless network while providing the speed for accessing large files in an office environment

Backbone: a large transmission line that carries data gathered from smaller lines that interconnect with it.

Encapsulation: the inclusion of one thing within another thing.

1.6 Hardware troubleshooting

REVISED

You must

- know about the process needed to troubleshoot common hardware problems
- know about the documentation required when troubleshooting common hardware problems.

Identifying hardware faults:
- start
- identify the problem
- define theory of possible cause
- test theory
- create a plan of action
- verify problem
- document results
- end.

Troubleshooting tools:
- software diagnostic packages that run predetermined tests on different hardware components within an IT system
- multimeter – checking the electrical values of the voltage
- cable tester – testing network cables
- POST card – plugs into an expansion slot of a computer and tests the operation of the system as it boots up.

Documentation/fault management:
- fault log – records information relating to the fault, for example what the fault is, when it occurred, where it occurred, how the fault was resolved and when
- test plans – test number, type of test, expected result, actual result, resolution, further test number
- manufacturer information relating to the faulty hardware
- technical guides used for researching similar faults and potential resolutions.

1.7 Units of measurement

REVISED

You must

- know about the units of measurement used in IT.

- **Bit**: abbreviation for binary digit (0 or 1); smallest unit of data in a computer.
- **Nibble**: equal to 4 bits or half a byte; can be expressed by one hexadecimal digit.
- **Byte**: equal to 8 bits; most computers use byte to represent a character such as a letter, number or typographic symbol.

Metric		Binary	
Kilo	(kilobyte) 1000 bytes	Kibi	1024 bits
Mega	1000 kilobytes	Mebi	1024 kibi
Giga	1000 megabytes	Gibi	1024 mebi
Tera	1000 megabytes	Tebi	1024 gibi
Peta	1000 terabytes	Pebi	1024 tebi

In 1998 it was decided that kibibyte would be used to signify 1024 bytes, while the kilobyte would be retained solely for 1000 bytes and so on.

1.8 Number systems

REVISED

You must

- know the different numbering systems.

- **Binary**: a numbering system that only uses two digits, 1 and 0. All information that is processed by a computer is a sequence of 1s and 0s. This means that all data to be processed by a computer needs to be converted into binary format. This is a base 2 numbering system.
- **Decimal**: a numbering system with ten digits as follows: 0, 1, 2, 3, 4, 5, 6, 7, 8, 9. All decimal numbers have a binary equivalent. This is a base 10 numbering system.
- **Hexadecimal**: a numbering system containing 16 digits as follows: 0, 1, 2, 3, 4, 5, 6, 7, 8, 9, A, B, C, D, E, F. Each hex digit reflects a 4-bit binary sequence. This is a base 16 numbering system.

You must

- understand how to convert between the different numbering systems.

Decimal (denary)	Binary	Hexadecimal
0	0000	0
1	0001	1
2	0010	2
3	0011	3
4	0100	4
5	0101	5
6	0110	6
7	0111	7
8	1000	8
9	1001	9
10	1010	A
11	1011	B
12	1100	C
13	1101	D
14	1110	E
15	1111	F

Convert decimal to binary

The easiest way to convert decimal to binary is by continually dividing the number by two. For example, to convert 37 from decimal to binary:

$37 \div 2 = 18$ remainder (R) 1

$18 \div 2 = 9$ R0

$9 \div 2 = 4$ R1

$4 \div 2 = 2$ R0

$2 \div 2 = 1$ R0

$1 \div 2 = 0$ R1

Working from the bottom up and looking at the remainder values, the binary equivalent is 100101.

Convert binary to decimal

To convert this binary number, 100101, back to decimal, work from the right-hand side and give each digit a place number as follows:

9	8	7	6	5	4	3	2	1	0
				1	0	0	1	0	1
				1×2^5	0×2^4	0×2^3	1×2^2	0×2^1	1×2^0
				32	0	0	4	0	1

The place number is the power of 2.

Therefore, $32 + 0 + 0 + 4 + 0 + 1 = 37$.

Remember that any number to the power of 0 equals 1, so $2^0 = 1$.

Convert decimal to hexadecimal

To convert a decimal number to hexadecimal, divide by 16. For example, to convert 37 from decimal to hexadecimal:

$37 \div 16 = 2$ R5

$2 \div 16 = 0$ R2

Working from the bottom up and looking at the remainder values, the hexadecimal for 37 is 25.

Convert hexadecimal to decimal

To convert from hexadecimal to decimal, follow a similar process to the binary to decimal conversion.

9	8	7	6	5	4	3	2	1	0
								2	5
								2×16^1	5×16^0
								32	5

Therefore, $32 + 5 = 37$.

Convert binary to hexadecimal

To convert binary to hexadecimal, you split your binary numbers into groups of four. If there are not enough binary numbers, you add zeros at the front. For example:

- the binary notation 10111001 would be split into 1011 1001
- the binary notation 101 would have an additional zero placed at the front to become 0101.

Place an 8 above the first digit, a 4 above the second digit, 2 above the third digit and 1 above the last digit, as follows:

0101 becomes: $0^8 1^4 0^2 1^1$

Each digit represents the power of 2. Therefore, from the first digit to the last:

$0 = 0$

$1 = 1 \times (2 \times 2) = 4$

$0 = 0$

$1 = 1 \times 1 = 1$

Therefore, 0101 becomes 0401. Now, add the four numbers together as follows:

$0 + 4 + 0 + 1 = 5$ in hexadecimal

When you have longer binary numbers you convert one four-digit group at a time. For example, if you had 0010 1001:

0010 becomes $0^8 0^4 1^2 0^1 = 0 + 0 + 2 + 0 = 2$ in hexadecimal

1001 becomes $1^8 0^4 0^2 1^1 = 8 + 0 + 0 + 1 = 9$ in hexadecimal

Therefore, 101001 in binary is 29 in hexadecimal.

Convert hexadecimal to binary

To convert hexadecimal to binary, you first convert the hexadecimal number into decimal and then into binary. For example, to convert 29 in hexadecimal:

9	8	7	6	5	4	3	2	1	0
								2	9
								2×16^1	9×16^0
								32	9

$32 + 9 = 41$ (hexadecimal converted to decimal)

Then, converting 41 decimal into binary:

$41 \div 2 = 20$ R1

$20 \div 2 = 10$ R0

$10 \div 2 = 5$ R0

$5 \div 2 = 2$ R1

$2 \div 2 = 1$ R0

$1 \div 2 = 0$ R1

From the bottom to the top the binary equivalent is 101001.

Now test yourself

TESTED ☐

Convert the following:

Decimal	Binary	Hexadecimal
47		
264		
92		
45		

Binary	Decimal	Hexadecimal
101110		
11111		
101010101010		
1100111100		

Hexadecimal	Binary	Decimal
D5CF		
3FA7		
FFFF3		
A8		

LO2 Understand computer software

2.1 Types of software

You must

- know about different types of software and their characteristics
- understand the use of different types of software
- justify the types of software to use within a given context.

Type of software	Characteristics	Uses/justification
Open source Used by companies such as Twitter, Facebook and the BBC Examples: Python, Mozilla Firefox, Google Chrome, MySQL, GIMP, Linux	Users have the right to run the software, inspect, modify and distribute the source code/software Little or no licensing cost Can be used on multiple systems with no restrictions	Flexible and can therefore be used and changed as required to meet specific needs More likely to provide what the end user needs because the people developing it are usually end users themselves
Closed source Examples: Microsoft Office, Adobe Acrobat, McAfee antivirus software, Dreamweaver	Software distributed under a licence agreement to authorise users with private modification, copying and republishing restrictions Not distributed in the public domain	Common software used on home and business computers and therefore technical support is available Constantly updated to mitigate potential security breaches
Off-the-shelf	Designed for a wide range of consumers with a standard design and framework Cheaper to build than bespoke software May need to pay for updates Updates may be for a limited period only and therefore can become obsolete	Software commonly used in homes and businesses, e.g. word processing, spreadsheets, databases, desktop publishing, graphics
Bespoke	Designed to meet the specific needs of a business More expensive to build Will be updated based on the budget and requirements of the business Although upfront costs are more expensive there are no licensing costs Continually dependent on the developer	Offers huge commercial and business benefits, giving a 'competitive advantage'

Type of software	Characteristics	Uses/justification
Shareware	Provides you with an opportunity to try before you buy You get a more personal service from the developers Cheaper than off-the-shelf packages Software is scanned by the authors and shareware sites for viruses Shareware is widely available	Used by businesses to be able to 'try before they buy'
Freeware Examples: Adobe Reader, Skype, Wix	Copyrighted by the developer Developer retains the right to control distribution, modify and sell the software Distributed without its source code Can be downloaded, used and copied without restrictions	Useful for small/new businesses to use without additional expense for software
Embedded	Used to control machines or devices not typically considered as computers Specialised for the particular hardware that it runs on Has time and memory constraints Can standalone or interact with a larger system via a communication channel such as internet, Bluetooth, etc.	Used in: ● cars, e.g. anti-lock brakes ● aerospace ● banking, e.g. teller machines ● security ● autofocus cameras ● automatic toll systems for roads ● elevators ● power supplies ● GPS ● washing machines ● microwaves ● embedded OS systems, including IOS used in Apple products

Now test yourself

TESTED ☐

1 A small business is not sure which software would be best for them to use and someone suggested that they try shareware software. They have asked for your advice in deciding whether to try a shareware application, have one designed specifically for them, or buy an off-the-shelf package.
Provide the business with a justification for the use of each of these types of software.

2 Explain the two characteristics of embedded software.

3 Identify one use for embedded software.

4 A large organisation requires a software application that needs to be tailored to their specific requirements. What type of software would you recommend to the organisation and why?

2.2 Applications software

You must

- know about the different software applications available
- understand the purpose of each application
- understand the advantages and disadvantages of each application.

Classification	Advantages	Disadvantages	Purpose
Productivity software			
Word processor	Easy to correct mistakes Can save multiple versions of a document Includes a spelling and grammar checker Formatting enables pages of documents to be presented so that they are more appealing or easier to read Can mail merge with a database to send the same letter to multiple people Copies can be made, saving on printing costs	Data can be lost or corrupted Some symbols are not easily accessible Requires a suitable system to be available so that they can be edited and viewed 'on the go'	Used to create, manipulate, format, store and print text
Spreadsheet	Makes calculations easier to perform and understand Reports can be formatted easily by hiding rows and columns Can increase productivity using templates Can interact with databases to populate reference fields Integration with graphic and word processing applications improves the production of reports and graphs, making figures easier to explain	Deskilling workers as they no longer require specialist skills Individual users can 'hoard' data by creating individual spreadsheets stored on individual PCs Can result in a duplication of data and effort Spreadsheet structure can increase storage requirements over the needs of raw data	Used for the organisation, analysis and storage of numerical data in columns and rows

Classification	Advantages	Disadvantages	Purpose
Database	Reduces data redundancy Reduces updating errors Increases consistency with presentation of data Greater data integrity Improved data security Reduced data entry, storage and retrieval costs Improved data sharing Improved decision making due to generation of better-quality information Increased end user productivity	Complex, difficult and time-consuming to design Can require substantial hardware and software costs Conversion costs when moving from a file-based system to a database system Initial training required for developers and users Maintaining currency of data	Used for the creation, updating and reporting of data Manages the collection of data Can be used to track orders, staff holidays, stock control, hotel bookings, etc.
Email	Email is delivered extremely fast Available 24 hours a day, 365 days a year Webmail can be sent and received from any computer with an internet connection, regardless of location Email is free if using broadband An email can be sent to multiple people at the same time Cheap – the cost is the same regardless of distance and the number of recipients Permanent – a record of messages and replies can be retained Can send attachments such as documents, images and diagrams	Recipient requires internet access to receive mail Viruses can be spread through email attachments Phishing attacks No guarantee that the email will be read Spam – junk mail, unsolicited mail Can send emails to an incorrect person in error, potentially divulging confidential/sensitive information or data Can require a lot of electronic storage space	Used for communication by individuals and businesses
Development tools			
Compiler	A program that is compiled is a self-contained unit that is ready to be executed, so it runs faster	Compilers are hardware specific It can take time to compile large programs	Used to convert instructions into machine code or lower-level object code so that they can be read and executed by a computer system; a compiler translates the entire program before it runs

→

L02 Understand computer software

Classification	Advantages	Disadvantages	Purpose
Debugger	Works step by step through the code Stops at the point where an error has occurred, enabling investigation and correction of errors Attached to an already-running program	Does not run in **real time**, so may not expose all problems	Used in the detection and correction of errors in other computer programs
Translator	Syntax and execution errors are quicker to identify as it works through the code one line at a time It will stop at the end of the line containing the error	Slower to execute than a compiled program as it must translate the source code every time it is run	Used to read, translate and execute one statement at a time from a high-level language program into an equivalent program in a different computer language
Integrated design environment (IDE)	Allows for greater collaboration between a group of programmers working on the same project Increases efficiency as the resources required are within one environment Improves project management by forcing developers to write comments in different areas	Too complex for novice programmers Each IDE has its own unique learning requirements, therefore time will be required to learn them Unable to automatically correct errors, so it's still a requirement to be able to code efficiently	A software suite that includes the basic tools developers require to write and test software An IDE is a code editor, compiler or interpreter and debugger that can be accessed through a single graphical user interface
Business software			
Management information system (MIS)	A single integrated system allowing for improved communication between relevant personnel Helps better decision making	The quality of the system is dependent on the quality of the data; inaccurate data presents inaccurate information, which can have a negative impact on decision making Security issues; robust security measures need to be implemented, which can have an impact on the finance and operation of the organisation	A combination of computer hardware and software used to gather relevant data internally and externally to an organisation The data is processed, integrated, stored and constantly updated; it is made available to authorised personnel in a form that meets their needs

Classification	Advantages	Disadvantages	Purpose
Multimedia	Multi-sensorial: uses a number of senses, e.g. hearing, seeing, talking Integrated: the different mediums are combined into one process Flexible: can be changed to adapt to different situations and audiences	Accessibility: requires a system and power to operate that may not be available in some locations Distracting: may take away from the focus of the communication Costly: made up of more than one medium Time-consuming: it takes time to create as using more than one medium Takes time to learn to do well	Used to combine sound, images, video and text, e.g. for websites, presentations, games
Collaboration	Efficiency enables team members to work together regardless of their location Can be accessed 24/7 as long as internet access is available Cost-efficient as team members can access it from different locations and do not have to travel Makes project management easier	Can reduce personal contact between team members as all communication is online Network and equipment failure can cause delays	Used to manage, share and process files, documents and other types of data from multiple users and systems at any time and anywhere
Project management	Real-time collaboration Sharing of documents, files, etc. Aids cost management Reporting can be streamlined to only include data required for specific milestones and reporting purposes Aids the management of risks, forecasting and budgets	Can be costly May overly complicate simple projects Can take time to learn due to its complexity Access control: consideration needs to be given to who can access and what can be accessed	Used to improve the efficiency of a project team Used to track the implementation, progress and completion of a project

LO2 Understand computer software

➔

Classification	Advantages	Disadvantages	Purpose
Manufacturing	An integrated system can lower IT costs and improve efficiency A single system can reduce training requirements for end users (only one system to learn) Total visibility of all business data Improved reporting and planning Improved collaboration and workflow Improved data quality and accessibility	Can be costly to purchase Downtime due to network and system issues	Used for scheduling, purchasing, shipping, customer management and accounting for a manufacturing organisation
CAD/CAM	CAD: ● enables design changes to be made rapidly ● enables the designer to check that the design is within specification ● enables clients to view designs at an earlier stage in the design process ● reduces human error CAM: ● enables designers to construct physical prototypes during the design process ● enables clients to check the progress of functional and semi-functional prototypes at an earlier stage ● large-scale production results are consistent ● speeds up production of low-volume products ● enables high levels of accuracy	CAD: ● software complexity – difficult for first-time users to learn ● training costs can be high ● software consumes large amounts of computer processing power ● requires high-quality computer hardware, which can be costly CAM: ● software complexity –difficult for first-time users to learn ● training costs can be high ● requires advanced manufacturing devices, which are expensive	CAD is used for designing and documenting products CAM is used to program the manufacturing process
Publishing	Text can be formatted using a wide range of fonts, effects and colours Background colours can be changed for blocks of text and images Text can be wrapped around images Page layout templates can be set up so that each page looks the same	Software can be complex, requiring training Training takes time and costs money	Used to create page layouts when combining text and graphics, e.g. newspapers, leaflets, newsletters, magazines, books, posters, business cards, greeting cards, web pages

Classification	Advantages	Disadvantages	Purpose
Expert systems (computer programs that use artificial intelligence)	Can process large amounts of information Provides answers for repetitive decisions, tasks and processes Reduces time required to solve problems Reduces the amount of human error Takes into consideration factors that human experts may not consider Knowledge can be updated and extended Can be used in dangerous, hazardous environments	Lack of creative response available from human experts Difficult to automate complex processes No flexibility; they need to 're-learn' when adapting to rapidly changing environments Not able to recognise that there is no answer to a problem Unable to explain logic or the reason behind a decision Does not learn from mistakes Cannot create new solutions	Software that is capable of intelligent behaviour, e.g. voice and image recognition software
Healthcare	Can improve patient satisfaction Aids the diagnosis of patient symptoms	Requires training to use Cost of training and training time required Impact if system goes down	A wide variety of healthcare software is available and used for different purposes, e.g. MIS, imaging and visualisation (X-rays, CT and MRI scans)

Now test yourself

TESTED

1 An organisation wants to store the information collected from an online survey. This includes the name and address of the person completing the survey as well as their answers to the questions. Which application software would you recommend they use? Justify your answer.

2 What is the difference between a compiler and a translator?

3 A project manager has a team of software developers who all work remotely. What business software would you recommend they use to help them work on a project together effectively and to keep track of how the project is progressing? Justify your choices.

4 Discuss the advantages of using CAM for a manufacturing process.

Real time: a level of computer responsiveness that a user senses as sufficiently immediate or that enables the computer to keep up with some external process.

2.3 Utility software

You must

- understand the purpose of a variety of utility software
- understand the advantages and disadvantages of different utility software.

Utility software	Purpose	Advantages	Disadvantages
Backup	Used to back up files, folders, documents, software data and even entire computer systems		
	Full backup: • allows for the complete restoration of all backed up files	Full backup: • faster restore time	Full backup: • backup time is slower • storage space requirements are larger if more than one copy is retained • security issues – if the backup media is illegally accessed through theft or **hacking**, it provides access to a copy of the entire data held by a business
	Incremental backup: • only backs up the files that have changed since the most recent backup	Incremental backup: • faster backup time; lower storage space requirements	Incremental backup: • slower restore time as each incremental backup has to be restored
	Differential backup: • backs up all files that have changed since the last full backup	Differential backup: • restore is faster than incremental backup • backing up is faster than full backup • storage requirements are lower than full backup if more than one full version is retained	Differential backup: • restore is slower than restoring from a full backup • backing up is slower than an incremental backup • storage space required is more than an incremental backup
	Mirror backup: • a copy of selected folders and files at a given point in time • will only copy new and modified files after the first copy has been made • deleted files will be removed from the mirror backup as well as the original	Mirror backup: • creates a snapshot of selected files and folders in a destination that you can browse and access later without the need to run a backup manager	Mirror backup: • unable to track different versions of files

Utility software	Purpose	Advantages	Disadvantages
Antivirus	Scans files and systems to check for threats and infections that could result in a breach of security to the system Responds to threats and infections on the system by quarantining infected programs Protects the computer system from viruses by scanning downloads and attachments Runs in the background when the user is on the internet Protects against spyware and adware	Decreases the chances of the computer system getting infected from viruses Helps to prevent **hackers** from gaining access to personal/sensitive information If it includes a **firewall**, it will block unauthorised incoming connections Protects against spyware and identity theft Protects from spam emails	They do not always use all the different detection methods The installation and use of antivirus tools can consume large amounts of computer resources and memory space on the hard drive, causing the system and network connection to slow down
Compression	Used to increase the efficiency of file storage and backup Used to post files on a web page for download by end users Used to send large documents as an email attachment	Used to compress multiple files into one smaller file Less disk space for storage Increases reading and writing time to system Faster file transfer	Compressed files must be uncompressed to be accessed A recipient of a compressed file must understand how the file(s) was compressed and have the tools available to decompress it

Now test yourself

TESTED ☐

1 Compare and contrast the advantages and disadvantages of the various backups that can be made.
2 What is compression software used for and what are the advantages of using it?

Hacker: someone who gains unauthorised access to a computer system/network.

Hacking: method of gaining unauthorised access to a computer system/network.

Firewall: software designed to protect a computer system/network from unauthorised access.

Unit 1 Fundamentals of IT

You must

- know the different forms of operating systems and their key functions
- understand the benefits and limitations of each type of operating system.

Type of operating system	Features	Benefits	Limitations
Single user (e.g. home computer or mobile phone)	Provides facilities to be used on one computer by one user Supports more than one profile	Easier to maintain and debug Supports one user at a time Fewer requests for hardware and software, so less risk of damage to the system	Tasks take longer to complete Idle time is higher
Multiuser (tends to be used on network systems)	Designed for more than one user to access the computer at the same or different times Linked to a network so it can be accessed remotely More complex than single-user operating systems	Each user can access the same document or different documents on their particular PC at the same time If one computer in the system has an issue, other computers are not necessarily affected	Complex to set up If one computer attached to the network is attacked by a virus, it can spread to other computers on the same network Greater security required to prevent unauthorised access to data
	Single processor: ● performs one process at a time ● carries out the next process in the queue when the current process is completed ● suitable for general-purpose computers	Single processor: ● time-slices are short and give the user the impression that their programs are running continuously	Single processor: ● slower processing time than a multiprocessor operating system ● costs more because each processor requires separate resources ● less reliable as a failure of the processor will result in the failure of the entire system
	Multiprocessor: ● two or more processors will be in close communication with each but will share the same power supply, memory and storage	Multiprocessor: ● more work can be done in less time ● failure of one of the processors will not affect the overall functionality of the system	Multiprocessor: ● more expensive ● complex operating system required ● large main memory required ● feed can be affected if one processor fails

Type of operating system	Features	Benefits	Limitations
Off-the-shelf	Ready-made and available for sale to the general public, e.g. Microsoft Windows	Available immediately Upgrades available Compatible with hardware already acquired Less training required Development cost is shared	May require an annual fee May have a lot of features not required May not fully meet the needs of the end user
Open source, e.g. Linux	Source code is made available for use or modification as and when required by users and developers	Usually free (or cheap) Continually being improved No hidden costs Increased security – white hat hackers have contributed to the overall security	More difficult to find application packages to suit individual needs Not all hardware manufacturers develop drivers for open source operating systems Support is not free and must be paid for
Bespoke	Designed to meet the specific needs of a business	Will be updated based on the budget and requirements of the business Although upfront costs are more expensive, there are no licensing costs	More expensive to build Continually dependent on the developer

Now test yourself

TESTED

1   Explain the benefits and limitations of using an open source operating system.
2   Compare and contrast single processor and multiprocessor operating systems.
3   Identify two benefits to a business of using an off-the-shelf operating system.

You must

- know about the different types of communication methods
- understand how they are used within a business context
- know the characteristics of the different communication methods
- understand the purpose of the different communication methods
- understand the advantages and disadvantages of each method.

Communication methods	Purpose	Advantages	Disadvantages
Short Message Service (SMS)	To communicate with individuals instead of making phone calls, e.g. to confirm an appointment, to update a remote-working employee on an impending meeting	Convenient (can be sent any time, day or night) Time saving Respond when convenient	Messages must be short People respond negatively to unwanted texts Need permission to send texts to other people Must comply with data protection and privacy rules
Email	Used to communicate with customers, suppliers, service providers and colleagues in a business environment	Messages can be forwarded and redirected One email can be sent to multiple recipients Message can be easily filed and retrieved Email addresses can be stored in an address book Automatic notification if email not delivered Automatically date- and time-stamped Signatures can be set up Files, graphics and sound can be sent as attachments Convenient (can be sent at any time of the night or day and on any day of the week) Cheap method of communication	Must have internet access Spam emails can be received Risk of viruses from email attachments Emails can be sent to the wrong person in error and therefore confidential/sensitive data and information can be leaked Data storage can be a problem when large attachments are distributed

Communication methods	Purpose	Advantages	Disadvantages
Messaging software	Can improve customer service as it may be easier for them than taking a phone call Can be used for internal communication within a business Can be used for sales where a customer will message a business	Cost effective (online chats as opposed to the cost of telephone calls) Encourages efficient communication – encourages short, concise messages Mobile – can be used on both desktop and mobile devices with messages being synced across devices Works in real time Takes place in private between two users	Distraction – employees will stop what they are doing to read and respond to a message as it appears Can have security issues with malicious users exploiting software vulnerabilities to gain unauthorised access to computer systems Compatibility issues – not all users use the same system Archiving is not always available or, if it is, not simple to use
Social networking/ social media	Used to communicate with current and potential customers Used for marketing and market research	Reduces marketing costs Increases traffic to business website Increases sales Improves ranking on search engines Improves access to international markets Improves customer engagement Can be used to gather customer feedback Can be used to conduct market research	Requires a clear marketing or social media strategy to access the benefits Additional resources may be required Requires daily monitoring Risk of unwanted or inappropriate behaviour Risk of negative feedback, information leaks and hacking
Voice over Internet Protocol (VoIP) Examples: Skype, Google Talk, MSN Messenger	Used for making phone calls over the internet or LAN	Cost: initial set-up costs and ongoing costs generally less than a traditional phone line Accessibility: available at any location where both parties have an internet connection Flexibility: not limited to a certain number of phones as a normal telephone system can be Voice quality: with a reliable internet connection, voice quality is as good as, if not better than, a telephone Extra/less expensive features, e.g. call forwarding, call waiting, voicemail, caller ID, three-way calling	Reliable internet connection required with sufficient bandwidth Power outages or emergencies: if there is no power, there will be no internet connection; emergency services can find it difficult to trace calls on a VoIP system Latency: calls may appear to lag or delay due to latency issues

→

Communication methods	Purpose	Advantages	Disadvantages
Personal assistant	Can be used to: • organise and keep track of appointments • send and receive emails on the move • view documents on the move • make telephone calls	Lighter in weight than a laptop and easier to carry around Information can be uploaded from computers to PDAs or downloaded from PDAs to computers Music can be stored and played Can be used for presentations Can be used as GPS device If internet access is available, emails can be sent and received and the web can be surfed Handwriting recognition using a stylus and appropriate software Some devices can be voice activated	Not designed for rough use Small screens and can be difficult to navigate Additional costs besides paying for the device, e.g. the contract for using it as a telephone, data access Can be a distraction, e.g. surfing the web, making phone calls that are not work-related or playing games
Teleconference	Used for group meetings	Reduces the cost of group meetings Can attend meetings remotely Reduces travel expenses Reduces time required for travel Meetings can be scheduled ahead of time Encourages greater contact with other branches of the business Increases productivity by eliminating time and location barriers	Technical failures with equipment including connections prevents the teleconference from going ahead or from people 'attending' Unsatisfactory for complex negotiations and bargaining Impersonal and difficult to create group rapport Requires skills to use Difficulty in determining participant speaking order (one person may monopolise the meeting) Greater preparation required Informal
Video conference	Problem investigation without visiting the site of the problem Collaboration Visual and verbal communication with others	Similar advantages to teleconferencing except that there is a visual display as well, which can be documents, presentations, images and/or people	High-bandwidth communication link required Short time lag between speaking and receiving response High-quality dedicated video-conferencing systems are expensive to buy Similar disadvantages to teleconferencing

Communication methods	Purpose	Advantages	Disadvantages
Cellular	Mobile networks, e.g. mobile phones	Do not require a landline Greater mobility	Cost (purchase of a device and associated running costs) Loss of service based on location
Satellite	Access to customers and other businesses anywhere in the world	Broadband internet signals available from any location on Earth so useful for remote or rural locations Accessibility: useful for businesses with offices and/or customers around the world High bandwidth Coverage over a large geographical area Can be cheaper over long distances Quality of signal and location of sending and receiving stations are independent of distance	Slow connection (much slower than a dial-up connection) More expensive than other methods Can be affected by weather disturbances Time-lapse between sending and receiving Imperfect impedance may create an echo effect
Instant messaging	Enables internet chat conversations in real time Used to relay information back and forth	Cost: allows real-time communication between people anywhere in the world without paying international or long-distance charges when using the phone Convenient: not as intrusive as using the phone where someone would have to stop to answer it	Can increase the risk of virus attacks Can increase the risk of sensitive information being accessed by hackers Can create a distraction while a person is working on something else (tempted to read and respond)

Now test yourself

TESTED ☐

1 A retail manufacturer is considering using social media for digital marketing. Discuss the advantages and disadvantages of using this form of communication for marketing purposes.
2 An organisation wants to be able to communicate with its offices in more remote areas of the world, where standard internet access is a problem. What communication method would you recommend and why?
3 Explain the difference between teleconferencing and video conferencing.

2.6 Software troubleshooting

You must

- know about common software faults
- know about the tools used to investigate common software faults
- know about the documentation involved when troubleshooting common software faults
- understand how tools are used in different contexts and be able to justify their use.

Common faults

Unexpected software behaviour, for example:
- you click on a link and it does not work
- the browser suddenly closes and stops responding
- components of Windows or other programs no longer work
- you cannot start a program.

Software freeze, for example:
- system stops working when you try to open a program
- you have too many windows open and the system stops working
- system hangs due to driver-related issues, such as a video driver when you try to run a video or game.

Unexpected rebooting, which can be due to faulty hardware or installation of hardware causing issues.

Figure 1.3

Troubleshooting tools

For example:
- logs – records of previous issues and their resolution
- installable tools – virus checkers, software patches, registry cleaners
- baselines – snapshots of networks and the way they act normally.

Documentation

For example:
- logs
- manuals
- test results.

Now test yourself

TESTED

1 Your computer has random pop-ups showing on screen regardless of whether you are using a web browser or not.
What do you think is the cause of the problem, and what tools would you use to troubleshoot the problem?
2 Explain the use of baselines when troubleshooting software.

2.7 Protocols

You must

- know about protocols and their features
- understand the purpose of protocols
- understand the common usage of protocols in given contexts
- know the TCP/IP protocol stack and the common features of each layer.

Protocol	Purpose	Features
Internet Protocol (IP)	Method used to send data from one computer to another on the internet	Resides in the internet layer of the TCP/IP protocol stack
		Responsible for informing the PC, routers, switches, etc., where a specific data packet is going
		Universally addressed – IP defines the addressing mechanism for the network and uses these addresses for delivery purposes
		Connectionless protocol – it does not need to set up the connection between two locations before sending data
		Underlying-protocol independent – it allows transmission of data across any type of underlying network designed to work with the TCP/IP stack
Transmission Control Protocol (TCP)	Defines how to establish and maintain a network communication through which applications can exchange data Works with the IP	Resides in the transport layer of the TCP/IP protocol stack
		Point-to-point – a TCP connection has two end points
		Reliability – guarantees the delivery of data without loss, duplication or transmission errors
		Full duplex – end points can receive and send data simultaneously
		Connection oriented – the application requests a connection to the destination end point and uses the connection to transfer data
User Data Protocol or User Datagram Protocol (UDP)	Works similarly to TCP but without any error checking Used for live broadcasts and online gaming	Resides in the transport layer of the TCP/IP protocol stack
		Packets of data are sent to recipient without any check that the packets have been received
		No guarantee that all packets are being received
		No method available for requesting missing packets
		Communication is quicker than with TCP as no error checking takes place
		Used when speed is important and error correction not required

➜

Protocol	Purpose	Features
Simple Mail Transfer Protocol (SMTP)	Used for sending and receiving email Used in conjunction with POP3 or Internet Message Access Protocol (IMAP), allowing users to save messages in a server mailbox	Resides in the application layer Lacks built-in security features Mail relaying – able to relay mail from one server to another in line with set conditions Mail forwarding – under certain conditions an SMTP server will accept email from a non-local mailbox and forward it to the appropriate destination Mail gatewaying – some SMTP servers can be configured as email gateways Address debugging – the EXPN command can be used to determine the individual email addresses associated with a mailing list Turning – allows the SMTP sender and the SMTP receiver to change roles
File Transfer Protocol (FTP)	Used for transmitting files between computers over the internet using TCP/IP connections	Resides in the application layer of the TCP/IP protocol stack Relies on two communication channels between client and server: a command channel for controlling the conversation and a data channel for transmitting the content Allows a client to upload, download, delete, rename, move and copy files on a server A user of FTP usually requires a logon to the FTP server FTP sessions work in passive or active modes; passive mode requires the client to initiate all connections and therefore works well across firewalls and Network Address Translation gateways
Hyper Text Transfer Protocol (HTTP)	Foundation for data communication for the internet Used to deliver data on the world wide web (e.g. HTML files, image files, query results)	Resides in the application layer of the TCP/IP protocol stack Connectionless – the HTTP client (i.e. a browser) initiates the request and then disconnects from the server and waits for a response; the server processes the request and re-establishes the connection with the client Media independent – any type of data can be sent by HTTP as long as the client and the server know how to handle it Stateless – the client and server are only aware of each other during a request, afterwards they forget about each other; they cannot retain information between different requests across different web pages
Simple Network Management Process (SNMP)	Used to manage and monitor network devices and their functions	Resides in the application layer of the TCP/IP protocol stack Security – latest version includes authentication and **encryption** of SNMP messages as well as protecting packets during transit Provides a common language for network devices to relay management information within single- and multi-vendor environments in a LAN or WAN Very useful for large networks

Protocol	Purpose	Features
Internet Control Message Protocol (ICMP)	Used to report errors to protocol network devices to generate a message to the source IP address when there is a problem delivering IP packets	Resides in the network layer of the TCP/IP protocol stack Used for error and congestion reporting Integral part of IP
Post Office Protocol (POP)	Downloads email from a server to a single computer, then deletes it from the server unless settings are amended to include saving	Resides in the application layer of the TCP/IP protocol stack Only one computer can be used to check email Mail is stored on the computer used Sent email is stored locally on the PC, not on the mail server Easier to implement than IMAP More reliable and stable than IMAP Cannot access email account from multiple computers or devices and synchronise between them

TCP/IP protocol stack

Example

TCP use: when a web page loads, the computer sends TCP packets to the web server's address requesting the web page to be sent. The web server responds by sending a number of packets that the web browser puts together to form the web page and display it.

Example

FTP use: tends to be hidden behind the user interfaces of banking sites, as well as web browsers to download applications.

Example

ICMP use: used by network administrators to troubleshoot internet connections in diagnostics utilities including ping and traceroute.

Now test yourself

TESTED ☐

1 Describe SNMP.
2 Explain the purpose of an IP address.
3 What does the acronym HTTP stand for and what is its use?
4 Identify what resides in the application layer of the TCP/IP protocol stack.

Encryption: data is converted from a readable format to an encoded version that can only be decoded by another device if it has access to the decryption key.

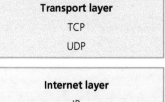

Application layer
SMTP
FTP
HTTP
SNMP
POP

Transport layer
TCP
UDP

Internet layer
IP

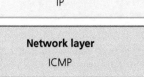

Network layer
ICMP

Figure 1.4 TCP/IP protocol stack

LO3 Understand business IT systems

3.1 Types of servers

You must

- know about different types of servers.

You need to be able to describe what each of the server types are used for.

Server type	Uses
File/print	Print servers are used to provide access to printers across a network. They support manageability for network printing and allow an administrator to control when print devices can be used by scheduling the availability of printers, setting priority for print jobs and configuring printer properties. An administrator can also view, pause, resume, and/or delete print jobs and manage printers remotely
	File servers are used to store data in a central location and must be kept secure to ensure that only those with authorisation are able to access the files
	File servers allow users to store their files remotely, rather than on their local hard disks, and share them with other users
Application	An application server is designed to install, operate and host applications and associated services for end users, IT services and organisations. It supports the hosting and delivery of high-end consumer or business applications
	An application server may be classified as a web server, database application server, general purpose application server or enterprise application (EA) server
Database	A high-end computer providing other computers with services relating to the access and retrieval of data from a database
Web	A computer system that hosts websites; it runs software allowing access to hosted web pages over the internet
Mail	A remote computer system that receives and delivers email messages for a client over a network, which is usually the internet
Hypervisor	Also known as a Virtual Machine Manager (VMM) allowing multiple computers to share a single hardware platform; it controls the operating system (OS) of each guest computer system

Now test yourself

TESTED

1. Describe the purpose of the file/print server.
2. Which server is used to install, operate and host applications and associated services for end users, IT services and organisations?
3. Describe the purpose of a mail server.
4. What is another name for a hypervisor server?

Hypervisor: hardware virtualisation technique enabling multiple operating systems to run on a single host system simultaneously.

3.2 Virtualisation

You must

● know about different forms of virtualisation
● understand the benefits and limitations to a business of using virtualisation technology.

> **Virtualisation:** creating logical resources from physical resources.

Remember that **virtualisation** is not the same as cloud computing. Virtualisation is software that manipulates hardware, while cloud computing is a service that results from that manipulation.

Type of virtualisation	Characteristics	Benefits	Limitations
Server	The partitioning of physical servers into multiple virtual servers, each running its own operating system and application; this makes each of the virtual servers look and act like a physical server to the end user	Reduction in capital outlay and operating costs Can minimise or eliminate downtime Increases IT productivity, efficiency and responsiveness Enables business continuity and disaster recovery Simplified data-centre management	Requires extra hardware resources Training required for the technical staff Complex system problems can be harder to analyse
Client	The operating system is managed centrally on a server and executed locally on a client device; a constant network is not required even though the disk image is updated and backed up using synchronisation with the server	The machines can be standardised and used across a large variety of different hardware configurations Easier to back up, secure, encrypt and repair disk images Easier to configure, deploy and manage More reliable and long lasting Minimal maintenance and, therefore, lower maintenance costs	Availability and performance depend on network/internet connection Multiple monitor connections may not be possible with some solutions or could be limited
Storage	Used for data storage management	Reduces the amount of physical storage required Simplifies and reduces the time required for backup, recovery and general storage activities	Can be difficult to solve problems when something goes wrong

→

Type of virtualisation	Characteristics	Benefits	Limitations
Cloud	The delivery of shared computing resources, software or data as an on-demand service through the internet	Outsourced IT – provided by a service provider Quick to set up Pay-as-you-go (e.g. SaaS – Software as a Service); you pay for what you need Scalability – can scale IT capacity on an 'as required' basis	Security risks Bandwidth issues No redundancy, so will require the purchase of a redundancy plan if there is a failure in the technology
Hybrid	Combinations of **paravirtualisation** and **hardware-assisted virtualisation**	Improves the reliability of virtual machines Improves performance and efficiency Combines the advantages of paravirtualisation and hardware-assisted virtualisation	Training required to implement and manage the environment Upfront costs

Now test yourself

TESTED ☐

1 Discuss the benefits and limitations of a client server.
2 A small business is trying to make a decision on whether to install a server and, if so, which type. They have increased the number of staff and now have three small departments, all of which need to share the same software and file information. They have been advised to consider a client server or the cloud.
Which of these servers would you recommend? Justify your answer.

Paravirtualisation: a guest OS is recompiled prior to installation inside a virtual machine allowing for an interface to the virtual machine that can differ from that of the underlying hardware.

Hardware-assisted virtualisation: architectural support facilitating the building of a virtual machine monitor that allows guest OS to run in isolation.

REVISED ☐

You must

- know about different networking topologies and their characteristics
- understand the use of a particular topology for a given context
- be able to justify the use of a particular topology in a given context.

Topology	Diagram	Characteristics	Uses
Peer-to-peer (P2P)		Two or more PCs share files and access devices such as printers without requiring a separate server computer or software Every connected PC is a server and a client Access rights are controlled by setting sharing permissions on individual machines If PCs on the network are slow, they will slow down the other machines Each computer must be backed up Data can be deleted by users easily No control over security	Small offices Home networks
Client server: Domain Name Server (DNS)		End users (clients) can access resources from a central computer called a server Server manages the network Server controls the security of the network Clients are dependent on the server All data is backed up on the main server Servers can be updated to improve performance Users require logins to access the network More stable than P2P	Any business where greater control is required for security of data and information

→

Topology	Diagram	Characteristics	Uses
Bus	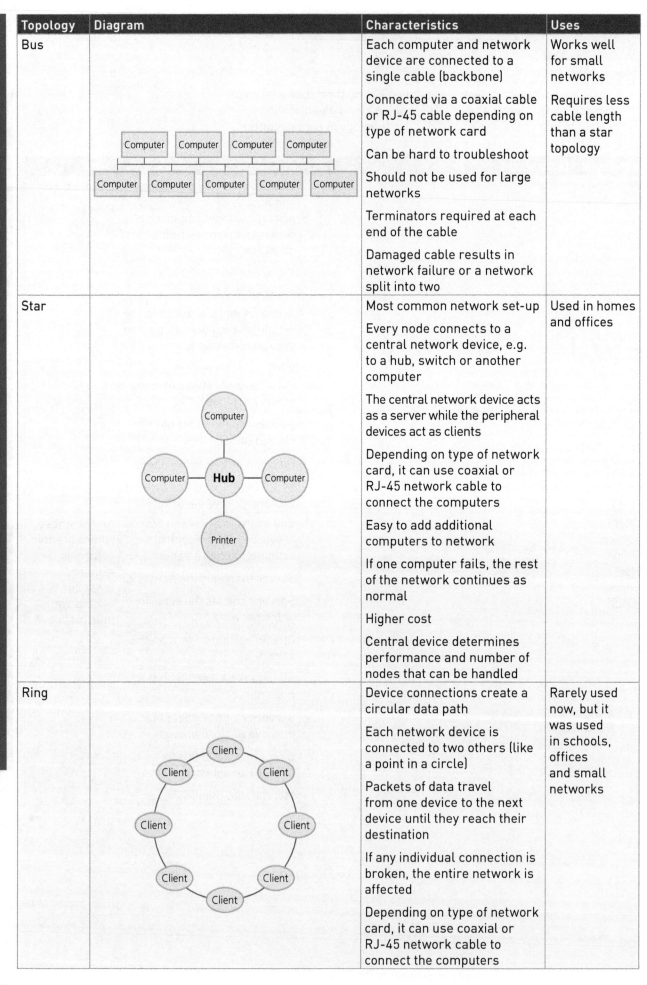	Each computer and network device are connected to a single cable (backbone) Connected via a coaxial cable or RJ-45 cable depending on type of network card Can be hard to troubleshoot Should not be used for large networks Terminators required at each end of the cable Damaged cable results in network failure or a network split into two	Works well for small networks Requires less cable length than a star topology
Star		Most common network set-up Every node connects to a central network device, e.g. to a hub, switch or another computer The central network device acts as a server while the peripheral devices act as clients Depending on type of network card, it can use coaxial or RJ-45 network cable to connect the computers Easy to add additional computers to network If one computer fails, the rest of the network continues as normal Higher cost Central device determines performance and number of nodes that can be handled	Used in homes and offices
Ring		Device connections create a circular data path Each network device is connected to two others (like a point in a circle) Packets of data travel from one device to the next device until they reach their destination If any individual connection is broken, the entire network is affected Depending on type of network card, it can use coaxial or RJ-45 network cable to connect the computers	Rarely used now, but it was used in schools, offices and small networks

Topology	Diagram	Characteristics	Uses
Mesh	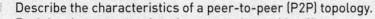	Not commonly used All network nodes are individually connected to most of the other nodes Each connection can carry its own data load Robust Faults are easily diagnosed Provides security and privacy Installation and configuration can be difficult Network can 'self-heal' if there is a breakdown, so no interruption of service to any node	The internet is the best example of a mesh network Used where locations do not have ethernet connections, e.g. outdoor concert venues, warehouses, transportation Useful where line-of-sight wireless signals are intermittently blocked Used for wireless networking as it is quick and simple to implement

- **Default gateway**: an access point or IP router used to send information from a computer on one network to a computer on another network or the internet.
- **IP address**: a unique address that different computers on a network use to identify and communicate with each other; each device on a network must have its own unique IP address.
- **Subnet mask**: a number that defines the range of IP addresses that can be used in a network.

Now test yourself

TESTED ☐

1 Describe the characteristics of a peer-to-peer (P2P) topology.
2 Explain why a star topology is commonly used in offices.
3 A business is rapidly expanding and needs to have greater control over the security of its data and information.
   Which topology would you recommend? Justify your answer.

3.4 Connectivity methods

> **You must**
>
> - know about the different connectivity methods and their characteristics
> - understand the purpose of different connectivity methods
> - understand how these would be used in a given context.

Local area network (LAN)

A **local area network (LAN)** is the networking of a group of computers within close proximity to each other, for example within the home, an office building or a school. It is usually used to allow the sharing of resources and services, for example files, printers, games, applications, email and internet access.

- **Ethernet**: the most widely installed LAN technology; a **link layer** protocol in the TCP/IP stack.
- **Token ring**: a LAN where all computers are connected in a ring or star topology and pass one or more logical tokens from host to host. Only the host that holds the token can send data. Tokens are released once the receipt of the data is confirmed.

> **Link layer**: the protocol layer that handles the moving of data in and out across a physical link in a network.

Wide area network (WAN)

A **wide area network (WAN)** is a network that spans large geographical areas, for example across cities, counties or countries. They can be private (for example when connecting the different parts of a business) or public. Think of the internet – this is the world's largest WAN. It connects lots of smaller LANs and/or MANs.

- **Asymmetric Digital Subscriber Line (ADSL)**: used for transmitting digital information at a high bandwidth.
- **Leased line**: a private bi-directional or symmetric telecommunications circuit between two or more locations. It is used by businesses to connect geographically distant offices and there is usually a monthly rental charge.
- **Integrated Services Digital Network (ISDN)**: a set of communication standards used for transmitting voice and data over a digital line. The digital lines are commonly telephone lines and exchanges and can carry voice (calls), data (internet), video (video conferencing) and fax information in the same line. Commonly used by the broadcasting industry, for example radio stations.

Metropolitan area network (MAN)

A **metropolitan area network (MAN)** is used to connect users with computer resources in a geographical area larger than that covered by a LAN but smaller area than a WAN, for example connecting networks in a city to create a single large network that could then be connected to a WAN more efficiently. It can also connect several LANs by bridging them using backbone lines; this sometimes being referred to as a campus network.

Voice

- **Public Switched Telephone Network (PSTN)**: the international telephone system that uses copper wire to carry analogue voice data. It consists of a collection of individual telephones that are hardwired to a public exchange. It allows subscribers at different locations to communicate by voice. Basically, a telephone system.
- **Cellular**: mobile phones use cellular telecommunications technology, a system that uses a large number of low-power wireless transmitters to create cells. Variable power levels allow cells to be sized according to the demand within a particular location. As a mobile user travels from cell to cell, the conversations are passed between each cell in order to maintain a continuous service.

Satellite

- **Voice**: a type of mobile phone used to connect to orbiting satellites, they are designed to work outdoors and in places where land-based terrestrial systems are unavailable. Journalists reporting from remote locations tend to use satellite communications.
- **Data**: this is where a satellite internet is created using a relatively small satellite dish on Earth that communicates with an orbiting **geostationary** satellite above the Earth's equator. Data is transmitted and received through the satellite internet. It only tends to be used if a business or person is located in an area where there are few internet connection options available. Any obstruction, poor weather conditions or poor latency will impact on the signal strength.

Figure 1.5 **Cellular communications transmitter**

Figure 1.6 **A satellite phone**

> **Geostationary**: moves in a circular orbit in the plane of the equator so that it appears stationary in the sky above a fixed point on the Earth's surface.

Now test yourself
TESTED ☐

1. A journalist is reporting on the impact of global warming on wildlife in a remote region of Africa.
   What would be the most appropriate connectivity method to use? Justify your answer.
2. An organisation has offices in various locations across the UK as well as abroad.
   What would be the most appropriate connectivity method to use? Justify your answer.
3. What does the acronym MAN stand for and what is it?

3.5 Business systems

You must

- know about different information systems
- understand the purpose of different business systems
- understand the benefits and limitations of each system in a given context.

Type of business system	Purpose	Benefits	Limitations
Management Information System (MIS)	To generate information to aid the process of decision making Plays a vital role in the management, administration and operation of a business	Integrated system supports improved communication Improves decision making	Data quality issues (how reliable is the data?) Security issues – sensitive data is a target for cyber criminals
Customer Relationship Management (CRM)	Provides an efficient system for the management and storage of information relating to potential customer leads Customer data generated through contact between the customer and the business is compiled across different channels, e.g. website, telephone, live chat, direct mail, social media	Helps maintain all customer data in one place, allowing workers to be more productive and efficient when tracking customer history etc. Helps to manage the growing database and speeds up the growth process Centralises data, enabling automatic emails and SMSs to be sent to customers Builds a long-lasting relationship with customers, e.g. sending them birthday wishes	Security issues – sensitive data is a target for cyber criminals Transition from a manual system to a digital system takes a lot of planning
Sales Order Processing (SOP)	Provides the tracking of data with respect to orders and inventory for every step of the process Order data is taken from the customer or customer service employee and stored in a central database Order information is sent to the distribution department and/or warehouse as appropriate	Speed of service Efficient and reliable order processing Fewer mistakes Integration with other key aspects of the business, e.g. finance and warehouse department	Security issues – sensitive data is a target for cyber criminals Sales could be lost if the system goes down, as people would shop elsewhere
Standard Operating Procedures (SOP)	Business system procedures specific to each organisation that describe the activities required to complete tasks in accordance with industry regulation and legislation as well as business standards	Fewer errors Increases efficiency and profitability Guidance on the resolution of problems	Does not always mean the same thing to different people (different interpretations)

Type of business system	Purpose	Benefits	Limitations
Help desk	Single point of contact for customers/users Used to gather information, which is used to determine who is best able to help the caller Help can sometimes be provided at the point of contact but may need to be escalated to others	Customers know where to go to get support Customer satisfaction – as long as they do not have long waiting times or are not dealt with by poorly trained staff Quality improvement – customer contact can be disseminated to relevant departments for review and consideration on how products and services can be improved Help desk staff can build up their skills and knowledge by supporting customers and can eventually provide fast response times for the customer	Staff must be trained to be efficient and supportive to customers Security issues – sensitive data is a target for cyber criminals Systems must be able to manage potentially large volumes of calls to avoid excessive waiting times for customers

Now test yourself

TESTED ☐

1 What are the benefits and limitations of using a CRM (customer relationship management) business system?
2 Explain the use of an MIS (management information system).
3 Discuss the benefits and limitations of help desk business systems.

LO4 Understand employability and communication skills used in an IT environment

4.1 Communication skills

You must

- know about different communication skills used in the IT environment and the potential barriers involved
- understand the different communication skills used for different audiences and situations.

Revision activity

You will have learnt about the different communication skills identified below. Complete the table with the information you have learnt about them. Some of them have been completed for you.

Communication Skill	Example	Used for	Potential barriers
Interpersonal skills		Skills used every day when communicating and interacting with other people both individually and in groups	
	Eye contact: looking at someone the same time that they are looking at you	When talking to other people in a face-to-face situation	Not being able to see the person/people you are speaking to clearly, e.g. during a video conference
	Body language: non-verbal communication skill where the conscious and unconscious movements and postures communicate feelings and attitudes		
Questioning techniques	Types include: ● open ● closed ● probing		
Verbal	**Meetings:** two or more people called together	Discuss/debate issues and problems and make decisions; can be face to face or remote	Remote meetings – poor video/audio signals, difficult to see/hear others
	Telephone: communication between two or more people who are not in the same room/location		
	Group discussions: gathering of individuals with a similar interest	To discuss ideas, solve problems, give comment; can be conducted face to face or remotely	

Communication Skill	Example	Used for	Potential barriers
Written		Most important and effective mode of business communication; involves the creation of a message using the written word	
	Report: a description of an event provided to another person(s) that was not present	For example, providing interested people with the results from an investigation	
	Letter: a communication addressed to a person or organisation		
	Email: message sent to one or more people electronically		
	Social networking: use of social media sites to interact with others		

Appropriate use of language

Type	Definition	Use
Formal	A form of communication where the dissemination/exchange of information is conducted through predefined channels	For example: requests, commands, orders, reports, providing information to a customer/client
Informal	Communication that does not follow any predefined channel	For example: casual discussion, sharing of feelings or ideas
Technical	A form of communication that includes technology-specific language or 'jargon'	Communicating technical or specialised topics Communicating using technology, e.g. help files, websites Providing instructions on how to carry something out regardless of how technical the activity is
Non-technical	A form of communication that is free from jargon and which a non-technical person could easily understand	Communicating something that is simple to understand Communicating technical information in a simple way without using technical jargon and terminology

Remember

When communicating technical information to a non-technical audience:
- Research the audience – what is it they need to know?
- What do you want your audience to do and/or understand?
- Keep it simple.
- Real-world examples bring things to life.
- Less is more.

Now test yourself

TESTED

1 You work in a computer store and have been asked to demonstrate how to use a webcam on a computer system to a customer. The customer has very limited IT expertise.
What type of communication skills would you use and why?
What type of language would you use and why?

REVISED ☐

You must

- know about the different communication technologies available
- understand the use of different communication technologies in a given context
- be able to justify the use of different communication technologies in a given context.

Type of communication technology	Uses and features
Presentation software	Used to display information; change/influence opinions; to appeal to emotions, feelings, values and thoughts of the audience
	Can include any combination of text, images, video, animations and sound, and link to other applications, documents, files, web pages
	Can use animation to enable aspects of the slide to appear when the presenter presses a button
Word processing	Used to type and edit text for letters, reports, memos, etc.
	Text can be formatted with font type, size and colour
	Can embolden, underline and italicise text
	Can create bulleted or numbered lists
	Graphics can be imported into a word-processed document
	Other features include cut, copy, paste, headers and footers, search and replace, spelling and grammar check
Email	A message, which may contain text and/or images and have attachments, sent through a network to a specified individual or group of individuals
	Can be sent anywhere in the world at any time
	Instant delivery
	Environmentally friendly
	Used for sending messages between colleagues, and between businesses and their customers
Web	Used to transmit and share information over the internet
	Used for e-commerce (internet shopping), booking holidays and travel, internet banking, providing information on products, general knowledge, etc.
Blogs/Vlogs	Blog – a list of journal entries posted on a web page: • entries are posted in reverse-chronological order • reflects the personality of the author or reflects the purpose of the website Vlog – a blog that includes video content (e.g. YouTube): • not usually created to make money • used for self-promotion, e.g. videos uploaded of people singing and playing an instrument • used for demonstrations on how to do something

→

LO4 Understand employability and communication skills used in an IT environment

Type of communication technology	Uses and features
Instant messaging (IM)	Used to exchange real-time messages through a stand-alone application or embedded software
	Takes place between two users in private, bidirectional communication
	You can usually see whether someone is online or offline and connect through a selected service (e.g. Facebook Messenger)
	Can include images and emojis in messages
	Some services enable users to send money via IM

There are many IM services available. It would be sensible to look at a variety and see what functions and features they provide, for example:

- Facebook Messenger
- Microsoft Skype (including Skype for Business)
- Google Hangouts
- WhatsApp Messenger
- Windows Live Messenger
- Yahoo Messenger
- WeChat.

Now test yourself

TESTED

1 You work for an IT company that has decided to provide customers with video clips on how to troubleshoot simple PC faults. You have been asked to recommend a communication technology to use. Which communication technology would you recommend and why?
2 You work on the customer help desk answering queries from customers with problems with their IT equipment. Which communication technologies could you possibly use and why?

4.3 Personal attributes

You must

- know about the different personal attributes
- understand why these attributes are important for certain job roles
- understand why these attributes are valued by employers.

Personal attribute	Definition	Important for these job roles	Reason for importance	Reason valued by employers
Self-motivation	Being able to do what is required without influence from others	Network manager IT technician Programmer Web designer Animator		
Leadership	Being able to motivate a group of people to work towards a common goal	Network manager IT technician Programmer Web designer Animator		
Respect	Regarding someone or something as being worthy of admiration because of their good qualities	Network manager IT technician Programmer Web designer Animator		
Dependability	Being reliable by always doing something that you say you will and not making promises you cannot keep	Network manager IT technician Programmer Web designer Animator		
Punctuality	Always being on time, e.g. attending a meeting or completing a task	Network manager IT technician Programmer Web designer Animator		
Problem solving	Being able to find solutions to simple or complex situations/issues	Network manager IT technician Programmer Web designer Animator		

L04 Understand employability and communication skills used in an IT environment

Personal attribute	Definition	Important for these job roles	Reason for importance	Reason valued by employers
Determination	Being able to work at something continually regardless of how difficult it is	Network manager IT technician Programmer Web designer Animator		
Independence	Being able to work without the control or influence of others	Network manager IT technician Programmer Web designer Animator		
Time management	Being able to use your time effectively and/or productively to ensure that work is completed on time	Network manager IT technician Programmer Web designer Animator		
Team working	Being able work with others to reach a common goal	Network manager IT technician Programmer Web designer Animator		
Written skills	Being able to communicate your message in the written form with clarity and ease regardless of the intended audience	Network manager IT technician Programmer Web designer Animator		
Numerical skills	Being able to reason with numbers and other mathematical concepts and then apply them to a range of contexts to solve a variety of problems	Network manager IT technician Programmer Web designer Animator		
Verbal skills	Being able to share information with others using speech, ensuring that the spoken words are understood, as well as using the correct enunciation, stress and tone of voice	Network manager IT technician Programmer Web designer Animator		

Personal attribute	Definition	Important for these job roles	Reason for importance	Reason valued by employers
Planning skills	Being able to make, develop and implement plans in order to achieve short- and long-term goals	Network manager IT technician Programmer Web designer Animator		
Organisational skills	Being able to use time, energy and resources effectively to achieve goals	Network manager IT technician Programmer Web designer Animator		

Revision activity

Complete the table above, stating why the personal attributes identified are important for the different job roles and why this would make them valued by employers.

Now test yourself

TESTED ☐

1 Identify the personal attributes required by a web designer.
2 Explain why the personal attributes you noted in question 1 are valued by an employer.

LO4 Understand employability and communication skills used in an IT environment

4.4 Ready for work

You must

- know about being ready for work
- understand why this is important for you and the organisation you are working for or applying to work for.

Figure 1.7 Ready for work

Revision activity

Look at the list of ways of being ready for work below. Consider how these aspects of personal presentation would be important for the different IT job roles covered in Section 4.3 above. Complete the table by noting why they are important to you and why they would be important to your employer in the relevant column.

Ready for work	Importance to you	Importance to your employer
Dress: • Appropriate clothing depending on job role		
Presentation: • Personal grooming • Appearance		
Attitude: • Can-do attitude • Responsiveness		

Now test yourself

TESTED

1 Explain why responsiveness and a can-do attitude are important to the job role of an IT technician.
2 You have been invited to an interview for a web designer. What dress code would you use and why?

You must

- know about different job roles in the IT industry
- understand the skills required for a given context.

Revision activity

You have already thought about personal attributes, which are non-technical skills required for the job roles in Section 4.3. You should now complete the table below by identifying the technical skills required for each of the job roles.

Job role	Technical skills
Network manager	
IT technician	
Programmer	
Web designer	
Animator	

Now test yourself

TESTED

1 Compare and contrast the technical skills required by a programmer and a network manager.
2 Justify the technical skills required for a job as a web designer.

LO4 Understand employability and communication skills used in an IT environment

4.6 Professional bodies and 4.7 Industry certification

You must

- know about different professional bodies and industry certification
- understand the purpose of professional bodies
- understand the benefits and limitations of membership for you
- understand the benefits and limitations of membership for an employer.

Professional bodies

Professional bodies are dedicated to the advancement of knowledge and practice of the profession (in this case, IT) through the development, support, regulation and promotion of professional standards for technical and ethical competence.

Examples of professional bodies for IT include:
- BCS (British Computing Society), the Chartered Institute for IT
- National Computing Centre (NCC)
- Society of Information Technology Management (Socitm)
- UK Web Design Association (UKWDA)
- Women in Technology
- Institute of Information Security Professionals (IISP)
- Institution of Analysts and Programmers (IAP)
- UK Information Technology Association (UKITA)
- Internet Advertising Bureau (IAB UK).

Membership	Benefits	Limitations
Personal	Professional recognition – confirmation of relevant experience, qualifications and skills (usually means you can add letters to your CV and business card) Provides you with information and advice, e.g. industry news, jobs, career opportunities Networking opportunities – attend local and national events and make new contacts Magazines – issue monthly or quarterly magazines that include industry news, articles and job vacancies Career development – offer career development programmes, training courses and assessments	Cost – membership can be expensive and must be renewed annually (some professional bodies provide a quarterly payment scheme) There are many professional bodies out there so it is important to research and select the one that will benefit you the most

Membership	Benefits	Limitations
Employers	Assurance of quality – proof that employees have the relevant technical experience and competence	Requires knowledge of the wide range of professional bodies and how employee membership will enhance the business
	Motivation of staff – investment in the training and development of employees make them feel valued	
	Continuous improvement – employees must commit to continuous professional development (CPD) to remain a member, so it helps to promote a culture of professional development in the workplace	
	Ethical standards – professional bodies commit to a code of conduct: to have regard for the public interest at all times, never to engage in corrupt practice or put the health and safety of others at risk; this shows that the employer also has ethical standards and is committed to a corporate social responsibility	

Industry certification

There are a wide range of industry (vendor) qualifications for the IT industry. The following are just some examples:

- Microsoft Certified Systems Engineer (MCSE)
- Microsoft Certified Systems Administrator (MCSA)
- Microsoft Certified IT Professional (MCITP)
- Microsoft Certified Technology Specialist (MCTS)
- Microsoft Certified Professional Developer (MCPD)
- CompTIA A+
- CompTIA N+
- CompTIA Security+
- Cisco Certified Internetwork Expert (CCIE)
- Cisco Certified Network Associate (CCNA)
- Project Management Professional (PMP)
- Certified Information Systems Security Professional (CISSP).

You do not need to know about the industry certification listed above in depth, but you do need to be aware of what is available and what areas of IT they relate to.

Now test yourself

TESTED

1 Explain the purpose of professional bodies in the IT sector.
2 You are employed as an IT technician and have been offered funding to study for industry qualifications such as CompTIA Security+ and CISSP.
Discuss the benefits to yourself and your employer of achieving these qualifications.

LO5 Understand ethical and operational issues and threats to computer systems

5.1 Ethical issues

REVISED

You must

- know about different ethical issues
- understand how different ethical issues can be addressed.

Ethical issue	Definition	Addressed by
Whistle-blowing	A current or past employee that reports the misconduct of an organisation. It could be something that has occurred in the past, is ongoing or planned for the future • **Internal whistle-blower**: reports misconduct to another person within the same organisation • **External whistle-blower**: reports misconduct to a person outside the organisation, e.g. the police or the media	Employees are protected from being fired or mistreated by law Organisations should have a whistle-blowing policy detailing what someone can expect if they report a concern
Disability/gender/sexuality discrimination	Being prejudiced against someone because of a disability, their gender or sexuality	The Equality Act (2010) protects a person from discrimination in the workplace and in wider society Organisations are required to adhere to the Equality Act 2010, providing evidence if required
Use of information	How personal information is gathered, stored, processed, used and disseminated	Organisations must comply with current legislation. The General Data Protection Regulation (GDPR) (EU) 2016/679 replaced the Data Protection Act (1998) in May 2018 Organisations must be able to show that they have a lawful basis for processing personal data
Codes of practice	A set of written guidelines or ethical standards that detail how people working in a particular job role/profession should behave	Codes of practice should be available to all employees within an organisation to ensure that they are aware of what is expected of them with respect to their conduct within the workplace

Ethical issue	Definition	Addressed by
Staying safe online	To maximise the personal safety of a user against security risks, to provide information and/or property associated with using the internet, as well as protection from cyber crime in general	Organisations should: ● provide training to employees ● ensure that systems and data are secure ● implement an online safety policy
Bias	To demonstrate prejudice against a person or thing in a way that is considered unfair	Organisations could: ● provide awareness training ● conduct a confidential survey of employees to find out if bias is occurring

Now test yourself

TESTED ☐

1 What should organisations have in place to provide details of how people should behave in work?
2 Explain the difference between an internal and an external whistle-blower.
3 Describe a situation in which someone may become an external whistle-blower.

> **Ethical issues:** used to create a moral and fair environment, to avoid discrimination and to promote a principled work ethic.

5.2 Operational issues

You must

- know about different operational issues
- understand how different operational issues can be addressed.

Operational issue	Definition	Addressed by
Security of information	Keeping data safe from unauthorised or unexpected access, alteration and/or destruction	Implementing a policy on who can view and update data and information
		Back up data regularly
		Implement guidelines for disaster planning and recovery
		Train employees with respect to security of data and information
		Implement risk assessments and protect systems and networks accordingly
		Compliance with legislation
Health and safety	Maintaining the health, safety and welfare of employees and, if appropriate, visitors to the premises	Complying with regulations for the use and position of screens and monitors (VDU regulations)
		Complying with office and workplace environment health and safety legislation when using computer systems
Disaster planning and recovery	Planning the recovery of data and systems in the event of a disaster, e.g. total system failure, cyber attack	Clear and decisive documented planning strategy to recover any loss to system and/or data
		Identification of roles and responsibilities of disaster recovery team
		Risk assessments identifying potential threats and vulnerabilities to systems and processes
		Dual networks (if one should fail, another is still available)
		Additional servers should one fail
Organisational policies	**Acceptable use policy (AUP)**: a document containing the constraints and practices that must be adhered to by a user in order to access a corporate network or the internet	Ensuring AUPs and code of conduct documents are available to all employees
	Code of conduct: a written series of rules, principles and values that serves as a framework for ethical decision making within an organisation	

Operational issue	Definition	Addressed by
Change management	A systematic approach to dealing with the change of an organisation's goals, processes or technologies	Implementing strategies for affective change, controlling change and helping people to adapt to change
		Implementing a procedure for requesting a change and for responding to requests for change, as well as following them up
		Being aware of the impact the change will have on the processes, systems and employees within the organisation
		Implementing a process for: ● planning and testing the change ● communicating the change ● scheduling and implementing the change ● documenting the change ● evaluating the effects of the change
Scale of change Drivers: ● change in business practice ● legislation ● competition Needs: ● improved networking ● remote access for employees	Reasons for an organisation making changes to their organisational goals, processes and/or technologies	Refer to section above Planning and communicating any change is key to its success

Now test yourself

TESTED ☐

1 Explain what is meant by the term 'scale of change'.
2 Explain the purpose of an acceptable use policy (AUP).

Change management: the systematic approach to dealing with change from the perspective of an organisation and individuals.

You must

● know about the different threats to computer systems.

Type of threat	Explanation
Phishing	Where a person is contacted (by email, telephone or text message) by someone posing as a legitimate organisation to encourage the divulging of sensitive information, e.g. personal information, banking and credit card details and passwords. This information is then used to access important accounts resulting in identity theft and/or financial loss
Hacking	This is the unauthorised intrusion into a computer or network system. ● **Black hat hackers** hack to take control over the system for personal gain by destroying, stealing or preventing authorised users from accessing the system ● **Grey hat hackers** hack into systems and then notify the organisations of the vulnerabilities within their systems, but do not have any malicious intent ● **White hat hackers**, also known as **ethical hackers**, only seek vulnerabilities when they are legally permitted to do so
Virus	Malicious code that replicates by copying itself to another program, boot sector or document and changes how the computer system works It requires someone to knowingly or unknowingly spread the infection. It can be spread via an email attachment, by clicking on executable files, visiting an infected website or viewing an infected website advertisement, and through the use of injected removable storage devices (e.g. USB drives) There are many different types of viruses
Trojan	A Trojan hides within what appears to be a harmless program or will trick a person into installing it. It collects information on the system, sets up holes in the security of the system or may take over the computer system and lock a person out. Trojans can affect the system in many different ways, including: ● manipulation of files to unite a group of victims' computers to form a **botnet** (backdoor) ● take advantage of vulnerabilities on the computer systems using programs containing data or code (exploits) ● a root kit is used to prevent malicious programs being detected so that they can run for longer on an infected computer ● Trojan-Banker – used to steal account data for online banking systems, e-payment systems and credit/debit card details ● Trojan-DDoS – attacks a targeted web address by sending multiple requests leading to a **denial of service (DoS)** ● Trojan-Downloader – downloads and installs new versions of malicious programs on to a computer ● Trojan-Dropper – used by hackers to install Trojans and/or viruses or to prevent the detection of malicious programs ● Trojan-FakeAV – simulates antivirus software; used to extort money in return for the detection and removal of threats even though they are non-existent ● Trojan-GameThief – steals user account information from online gamers ● Trojan-IM – steals logins and passwords from instant messaging programs ● Trojan-Ransom – modifies data on a computer system so that it no longer functions correctly, or data becomes inaccessible; the cyber criminal will restore your system's performance or unblock data for ransom money ● Trojan-Mailfinder – gathers email addresses from a computer system ● Trojan-Spy – used to spy on how a computer system is being used by tracking data entered via a keyboard, taking screenshots or obtaining a list of running applications

Type of threat	Explanation
Interception	When an unauthorised party has gained access to a system, resulting in the illicit copying of programs or data files, or wiretapping to obtain data in a network
Eavesdropping	The unauthorised real-time interception of a private communication, e.g. a phone call, instant message or video conference. It is used to access data, e.g. installing network-monitoring software (a sniffer) on to a computer or a server so that data can be intercepted during transmission
Data theft	The theft of data from a computer system or data intercepted during transmission across a network
Social engineering	This is when someone is manipulated into providing confidential information. Cyber criminals use social engineering to try and get information relating to passwords, bank information or to secretly install malicious software that will provide them with access to the information or to take control of the computer system

Ethical hacking: an attempt to penetrate a computer system/network on behalf of the owner in order to investigate security vulnerabilities that could allow malicious hackers to exploit it.

Botnet: a network system infected with malicious software allowing control without the owner's knowledge or consent.

Denial of service (DoS): an attempt to disrupt a network and/or organisation by issuing more requests than the system can cope with.

Now test yourself

TESTED

1 Describe what 'eavesdropping' is.
2 Explain the impact of a Trojan attack on a computer system.

5.4 Physical security

You must

- know about physical security measures and their characteristics
- understand why different physical security methods are used in different contexts
- be able to justify the use of different physical security methods.

Type of physical security method	Characteristics	Uses
Locks	Can be actual keys in a keyhole or a keycode for a door Requires policies to set out who has a key or keycode access	Used on server rooms in particular, and in any room where there must be restricted access to the computer systems Servers can be locked into racks that can be bolted to a floor Doors to empty offices should be locked Computers may have case locks that prevent unauthorised access to the inside of the system and prevent someone from stealing the hard disk Portable equipment should be kept in locked drawers, cupboards or safes Backups should be kept in lockable storage locations Printers should be in securely locked locations and bolted down so that they cannot be stolen
Biometrics	The measurement and statistical analysis of a person's physical and behavioural characteristics Used for identification and access to control Every person can be accurately identified by their intrinsic physical or behavioural traits Physiological identifiers: ● facial recognition ● fingerprints ● iris recognition ● retina scanning ● voice recognition ● DNA matching Behavioural identifiers: ● recognition of typing patterns ● other gestures, e.g. hand movements Biometrics are hard to fake Convenient as you cannot easily forget or lose a biometric like you can a password	Used to manage access to physical and digital resources, e.g. buildings, rooms and computing devices

Type of physical security method	Characteristics	Uses
Radio frequency identification (RFID)	Chip inside the ID badge contains information that is communicated to the scanner RFID badges have security flaws because they can be cloned	Can be used in ID badges to allow entry through keyless entry systems
Tokens	Sometimes called an authentication token Can be in the form of a smartcard or key fob Provides an extra level of security known as two-factor authentication User has a PIN that provides authorisation as the owner of the device; the device displays a number that uniquely identifies them as a user to the service, enabling them to log in; the identification number changes frequently Practical and easy to use	Small hardware device that is used to authorise access to a network service
Privacy screens	Quick and easy to install Maintains a clear view directly in front of the screen Blocks visibility when the display is viewed from a side angle Improved user comfort as reduces glare and eye strain Protects the screen from scuffs and scratches	Used anywhere where there is a risk that unauthorised personnel could view sensitive information on the screen, e.g. reception desk in a hotel
Shredding	Cross-cut shredders are the most effective as they shred paper into small squares and are therefore more secure Strip-cut shredders shred the paper into parallel lengths	Used for the destruction of physical documents

Now test yourself

TESTED ☐

1. What security measures would you use for a receptionist's computer that is on display in the reception area? Justify your choice.
2. Why are cross-cut shredders more effective when destroying physical documents as opposed to strip-cut shredders?
3. What is RFID?
4. Identify an item that many people have that uses RFID technology.

Biometric access: access to a computer system, network, room or building using technology that analyses human body characteristics for authentication purposes, for example fingerprints, retinas and voice patterns.

5.5 Digital security

You must

- know about digital security measures and their characteristics
- understand why different digital security methods are used in different contexts
- be able to justify the use of different digital security methods.

Digital security method	Characteristics	Uses
Antivirus	Any software that prevents unwanted access to a computer system and undesirable attacks from websites containing viruses Usually requires a licence fee if used for business purposes	Installed on to computer systems to prevent unauthorised access or risk of virus infection
Firewall	A software program or a piece of hardware that helps protect the computer system from hackers, viruses and worms from the internet Hardware firewalls are usually in routers to protect the network Software firewalls should be installed on individual computers	Hardware firewalls are used to protect networks and the computers that are on it Software firewalls should be installed on every computer so that each individual computer is protected in case one computer on the network becomes infected
Anti-spyware	Software that detects and removes spyware programs Monitors incoming data from emails, websites and downloads of files to prevent spyware programs from getting into the system Some anti-spyware programs only block spyware, others also block viruses Caution required as some alleged anti-spyware programs downloadable from the internet are spyware programs in disguise	Should be installed on computer systems to prevent the unauthorised collection of private and sensitive information via spyware programs hidden on the system Prevents the gathering of information such as internet interaction, keylogging, passwords, etc.
Username/ passwords	Passwords should be strong so that they cannot be guessed Ideally, they should contain a combination of digits and characters A username uniquely identifies someone on a computer system The combination of username and password is known as a login Login details are important targets for cyber criminals	Used to access, for example: ● computer systems ● email ● online banking ● e-commerce accounts

Digital security method	Characteristics	Uses
Permissions	Restricts access to information Can be set as read-only or read and edit Can restrict the deletion of files Can prevent the unauthorised installation of software Can prevent unauthorised access to certain websites Can prevent unauthorised access to personal email accounts, e.g. Gmail	Used to provide access rights to individuals to only the files/data/ information they require
Encryption	Transformation of information into a format that is unintelligible to anyone who does not have the correct key The sender and recipient must use the same algorithm Symmetric algorithms – the sender uses a shared secret key to encrypt the message; the recipient uses the same key to decrypt the message Symmetric **cryptography** is fast but unmanageable in a large system Asymmetric algorithms – the sender and recipient use related but different keys to encrypt and decrypt the message Asymmetric cryptography is slower but key management is simplified Folder encryption does not encrypt versions of documents and files stored in the 'temp' folder; deleting them is not sufficient protection	If an organisation runs a web server and deals in activities where there is sensitive information (e.g. banking, e-commerce), encrypted Hypertext Transfer Protocol Secure (HTTPS) connections should be used Used for encrypting files and documents while they are stored on a hard drive, removable media, in transit via email or the web Encrypting computers by encrypting the hard drives – authorised users are unaware as their login results in the contents they access from the drive being encrypted

Now test yourself

TESTED ☐

1 What is encryption and when would it be used?
2 Explain the difference between hardware and software firewalls.
3 Where would each type of firewall be used?
4 Explain what permissions are used for.

Cryptography: protecting data by encrypting it into a format called cipher text.

5.6 Safe disposal of data and computer equipment

You must

- know about the legislation for the safe disposal of data and computer equipment
- know about the different methods of safe disposal of data and computer equipment.

Remember

It is important that you know the current legislation for when you sit your exams. You will not be awarded any marks if you quote legislation that is out of date. The table below refers to legislation current as of May 2018.

Legislation

Environment Act (1995)	All redundant computer equipment (of no economic value) is classed as waste
	CRT monitors are classed as hazardous waste
	You must ensure your collection agents hold a Waste Carrier Licence
	You must ensure that your waste equipment goes to a licensed disposal site
	Your legal duty of care extends to when your equipment is reused, recycled or disposed of
Environmental Protection Act (1990)	Waste items must be assigned to registered carriers, properly stored and disposed of at appropriately licensed facilities
	Directors, managers and other employees who deal with environmental waste matters can all be held accountable, face fines and, in severe cases, imprisonment, if laws are broken
Hazardous Waste (England and Wales) Regulations (2005)	Since July 2005, most producers of hazardous waste in England and Wales have been required to notify their premises to the Environment Agency and register as a waste producer. A waste transfer note for hazardous waste should be issued by the licensed collecting agent at the time of collection.
Waste Electrical and Electronic Equipment (WEEE) directive	Sets criteria for the collection, treatment, recycling and recovery of waste electrical and electronic equipment
Landfill (England and Wales) Regulations (2002)	The standards set in relation to wastes that can go to landfill. The standards are called Waste Acceptance Criteria (WAC) and include hazardous waste

General Data Protection Regulation (GDPR) (EU) 2016/679	Replaced the Data Protection Act (1998), the content of which still applies
	Consumers can ask businesses and organisations for access to their personal data and for it to be wiped, giving them more control over how their information is used
	Personal data now includes IP addresses (used to identify a phone or computer visiting a website), internet cookies (data about your web-browsing habits) and DNA
	People have to opt in to being put on a cold-calling list and be made aware that their information is being passed on to marketing companies
	Individuals can demand that they are profiled by a person as opposed to a machine-based algorithm
	Consumers can move data between companies should they wish to, e.g. move photos between cloud storage companies
	It is now a criminal offence to identify people from anonymous data
	It is now a criminal offence if an organisation tampers with data that has been requested by an individual

Methods of safe disposal

- **Overwrite data**: a hard disk should be overwritten at least three times to ensure that the data cannot be recovered. This method allows you to reuse your hard drive.
- **Electromagnetic wipe**: also known as degaussing. This is where data is erased magnetically from magnetic storage media such as hard drives and backup tapes. The storage media is usually unusable after the data is destroyed.
- **Physical destruction**: storage media is totally destroyed, for example crushed using hydraulic apparatus.

Now test yourself

TESTED

1 An organisation has been contacting people on a cold-call list without their permission and passing their information on to other marketing companies. Which legislation have they broken and why?
2 What does WEEE stand for and what is its purpose?
3 What are the key points of the Environment Act (1995)?
4 An organisation wishes to permanently remove the data from some old hard drives before they are disposed of. Which data destruction method(s) would you recommend? Justify your answer.

LO1 Understand where information is held globally and how it is transmitted

1.1 Holders of information

> ### You must
> - know about the different holders of information, the category they come under and their possible locations
> - understand the access issues across the global divide.

Holders of information

- **Categories**: these can be individuals; businesses; educational institutions such as schools, colleges and universities; governments; charities; community organisations and health care services.
- **Location**: when considering the holder of the information, think about where they are located. Are they in the countryside or in a city or town? Are they in the workplace or at home? Are they in a developed country, such as the UK, or are they in a developing country, such as Ethiopia?
- **Comparison of technologies available and access issues**: consider what technologies are available to developed and developing countries, for example, UK has broadband in the vast majority of areas and fibre-optic broadband in many urban areas. Developing countries do not have the same broadband provision, so internet access is slow if available at all. What problems would this cause someone who was working in these different environments?

Global divide

The **global divide** refers to the ease with which a person or business can get access to the internet depending on their location in the world. Some countries have poor internet access or very limited access. It should also be remembered that even in the UK there are areas where internet access is difficult, for example areas in Gloucestershire, Cumbria, Somerset, Cornwall and parts of Wales.

> **Global divide:** the divide with respect to the access of information between different countries and different types of holders of information worldwide.

Figure 2.1 Access to communications varies from one region to another

Now test yourself

TESTED ☐

1 Explain what is meant by the term 'global divide'.
2 What do you need to consider when reviewing a particular holder of information?

1.2 Types of information storage media

REVISED

You must

- know about different types of information storage media and devices, and their characteristics
- understand their use and the advantages and disadvantages of each in a given context.

Storage media/device	Examples	Characteristics	Advantages	Disadvantages
Paper	Maps, forms, notes, tickets	Comes in different colours, weights, grades, sizes, brightness, reflectance, smoothness, grain	Very little energy is consumed when reading from paper Easy to use by people with limited computer experience Recognised and required by law; seen as being official and can be produced as evidence in court	Deteriorates over time Vulnerable to damage, e.g. fire, water Takes up a lot of storage space Recurring costs to purchase more paper Limited mobility; it is easier and quicker to send a document as an email attachment than to fax or post it Editing a document is not easy; originals need to be copied prior to editing to retain versions of a document Collaboration with others is not as easy as you would each have to work on copies of the documents
Optical media	CD-ROM, DVD-ROM, CD-R, CD-RW, DVD-R, DVD+R, Blu-ray™ Disc	Disks that are read by a laser Not based on magnetic charges like hard drives	Less likely to lose data Have a longer shelf life (around seven times longer than magnetic media such as hard drives) More durable than hard drives Cheaper to produce and therefore useful for backups and transferring small amounts of data between different computers	It takes more time to access information on different parts of the disk than a hard drive

Storage media/device	Examples	Characteristics	Advantages	Disadvantages
Magnetic media	Fixed hard drive	Disk surface (platter) coated in a magnetic film, which is where the data is stored Has read/write heads allowing data to be saved and used from the disc Use to store operating systems, software applications, files Used by real-time/online systems Used in file servers Storage from 250 GB to 4 TB	Processes data quickly Fast access speeds Easy to update/delete files Large storage capacities	Can be damaged easily Not portable
Magnetic media	Portable hard disk drive	Work in a similar way to fixed hard drives but connected to computer externally via a USB port Direct data access methods Storage from 250 GB to 3 TB Used to store large files (e.g. portable backup system) and to transfer data, files and software between computer systems via USB connectivity	Fast read/write times (direct data access) Large storage capacities Small and light, and has a protective casing, making it very portable Can be used on almost any computer via a USB port	Easy to misplace or have stolen due to its small size More expensive than other forms Can be damaged if dropped
Magnetic media	Magnetic tape	Tape is a thin strip of magnetic-coated plastic that is wrapped on to a reel Data stored in the form of binary numbers Data is written to and read from in sequence (in order, i.e. serial access) Sony developed a magnetic tape capable of storing 185 TB of data Used for backing up extremely large amounts of data Used for batch processing applications, e.g. producing payslips Used for backing up computer networks	Less expensive than hard disk drives Not easily damaged Very large storage capacities	Very slow data access rate and therefore not used for real-time applications Need an additional tape to update data

Now test yourself

1 What are the characteristics, purpose, advantages and disadvantages of the following solid state media?
- Solid state hard drives (SSD hard drives).
- Memory sticks/pen drives.
- Flash and micro flash memory cards.

2 A small business is considering changing from magnetic tape to a portable hard disk drive for their backups. Compare the advantages and disadvantages of each.

3 A business wants to provide their sales staff with a standard presentation to use as well as the relevant paperwork they need when visiting potential clients. Recommend an appropriate storage media, justifying your choice.

Remember

Refer to Section 1.2 of Unit 1, which also looks at different information storage media.

1.3 Types of information access and storage devices

REVISED

You must

- know about the different information access and store devices and their characteristics
- understand the purposes, advantages and disadvantages of each.

- **Hand-held device**: examples include small tablets, smartphones, wearable devices such as Fitbits and ebook readers.
- **Portable devices**: examples include larger tablets and laptops.
- **Fixed devices**: examples include desktop computers, smart TVs and game consoles.
- **Shared devices**: examples include cloud storage devices, database servers and data centres.

> **Remember**
> Refer to Sections 1.3, 3.1 and 3.2 of Unit 1, which also covers information about storage devices.

1.4 The internet

REVISED

You must

- know what the internet is
- know the characteristics of different internet connections.

The **internet** is a network of interconnected networks spanning the world. Different **types of internet connections** include:
- copper cable
- optical-fibre
- satellite
- mobile data networks
- microwave.

Different types of internet connections have different **characteristics**, such as speed, range (distance) and storage capacity.

> **Remember**
> Refer to Sections 1.4 and 3.4 of Unit 1 which also looks at the connectivity methods used.

LO1 Understand where information is held globally and how it is transmitted

1.5 World wide web (www) technologies

You must

- know about the different types of www network technologies and their characteristics
- understand the purpose of the different technologies in a variety of contexts
- be able to compare the different networks with respect to suitability for a given use, and any access issues related to each network.

Type	Purpose	Characteristics
Internet	Sharing of information	Open to anyone and everyone
		Collection of networks sharing information publicly in the form of interlinked web pages
		Internet protocol is used to define a site's unique location (seen as a domain name or URL)
Intranet	Allows people within the same company to share information over a LAN	Private with closed access
		Mainly used within businesses and organisations to provide access to files and applications among networked computers and servers
		May or may not have access to the internet
		Uses a firewall to prevent outside access to the intranet
Extranet	Allows collaboration and sharing of resources	Private with part-shared access
	Businesses use it to allow employees to log in to a virtual private network when they are not in the office	Similar to an intranet but is accessible via a web portal
		Can be accessed from anywhere
		User must have a valid username and password

Access issues

The main difference between all three is that the internet is public while the other two are very restrictive.

Home users use the internet when searching for and sharing information, and may use an intranet to share files between computers.

Businesses and organisations are the main users of intranets and extranets as a mechanism to restrict access to confidential data.

They all rely on the same TCP/IP technologies. They are different in terms of the level of access they allow to various users inside and outside of the organisation, as well as the size of the network.

Now test yourself

1 A business wants to provide its remote workers with access to their network system while away from the office. Which type of www technology would they use and why?
2 What are the main differences between internet, intranet and extranet?
3 Which type of system would home users use to share files between computer systems?

You must

- know the different **information formats** used on the world wide web
- understand the purpose of each format
- be able to justify the accessibility of each format to meet the needs of different holders of information.

> **Information formats:** the different ways in which information can be presented using www technologies, for example using social media and podcasts.

A **static website** is a website where the same content is displayed to all users viewing the website at the same time. It is a fixed website and the content does not change from user to user. A static website is a collection of HTML documents hosted on a server that are interconnected via hyperlinks.

A **dynamic website** has content that may change from user to user and/or from time to time. Dynamic web pages allow different content to be shown to each user. To do this, the components are stored separately at several stages and brought together into a common layout and transferred to the client browser. An application server and resources database are connected to the web server. When a request for a specific URL is made by the web browser, the web server receives and passes the information to the application server to provide the HTML file indicated in the URL. The application server brings out the layout required and fills it with the relevant content, for example text, photos, audio and video.

Web pages

Static web pages:
- have fixed content
- must be changed manually
- use only a web server
- are useful for websites where the materials and content rarely need to be revised or updated
- are quick and cheap to develop
- hosting is inexpensive
- browsing and loading is quicker
- created using HTML language.

Dynamic web pages:
- have changing content
- changes are loaded through an application where resources are stored in a database
- use a web server, application server and a database
- **client-side scripting** means that the web page changes according to a person's action on the web page; the content can be downloaded, modified and then uploaded
- **server-side scripting** means that pages change whenever a page is loaded, for example log-in and sign-up pages, application and submission forms, enquiry and shopping cart pages.
- created by using PHP, JavaScript and Actionscript languages.

Blogs

Uses:

- a diary to log personal experiences, opinions, thoughts and content
- for businesses to engage with their customers at a more informal level; a useful way to interact and engage with their target audience and to get feedback
- for photographers, film makers and so on to showcase their work
- to build a community to support the marketing of a business.

Benefits:

- helps to encourage audiences to a business' website
- each blog post creates one or more indexed pages on the website, which provides greater opportunities to show up in search engines
- converts the blog audience into potential new business leads.

Podcasts

- Provides the audience with a stronger connection with the presenter and, therefore, the business.
- Simple to use.
- Regular podcasts can promote brand awareness.
- Easy to archive and update.
- Reduces costs.
- Time-efficient form of communication (you can listen to them while doing other things).
- They are portable.
- On-demand technology – listeners can select what they want to hear and when.

Figure 2.2 **Podcasts**

Streamed audio and video

- Instant playback – files can be played almost immediately after they begin to download.
- Bandwidth can be a problem – if internet connection is poor, playback and/or quality is poor and interrupted.
- Provides protection from piracy. Files that are downloaded (especially copyright material) rather than streamed are easier to pirate and share with others.
- It is only accessible if the user is online; if there is no internet connection, then streaming cannot take place.

Social media channels

- **Social networks**, for example Facebook, Twitter and LinkedIn, are used to connect with people. They can be used for market research, brand awareness, customer service and to generate leads.
- **Media-sharing networks**, for example Instagram, Snapchat and YouTube, are used to share photos, video and other media. They can be used to promote brand awareness, audience engagement and other forms of marketing.
- **Discussion forums**, for example reddit, Quora and Digg, are used to share news, ideas, information and opinions. They are useful for market research.
- **Consumer review networks**, for example TripAdvisor, are used to search for and review businesses, products, brands, services, travel destinations, and so on. They are useful to promote a business and to resolve issues with unhappy customers.
- **Blogging and publishing networks**, for example WordPress and Tumblr, are used to publish content online. They are used by businesses to engage with their audience, build brands and generate leads and sales.
- **Social shopping networks**, for example Etsy, are used for shopping online, spotting trends, following brands and sharing finds. They are used by businesses to increase customer engagement and sell products via new channels.
- **Interest-based networks**, for example Houzz and Last.fm, are used to connect with others with the same interest or hobby. They are used by businesses to promote their products and services by engaging with their audience and building brand awareness.

Document stores

- A document store is also called a document database or document-oriented database. Some document stores may also be key-value databases. They are used for storing, retrieving and managing semi-structured data.
- They use documents as the structure for storage and queries.
- They contains a description of the data type and the value of the description.
- Data can be added by adding objects to the database.
- Documents are grouped into collections.
- They allow for flexible data modelling due to web, mobile, social and IoT-based applications changing the nature of application data models.
- Fast write performance.
- Fast query performance.

RSS feeds

- RSS is a type of web feed used to deliver regularly changing web content.
- It enables people to stay up to date with information they are interested in on the internet.
- It is an alternative communication channel – the more channels a business provides, the more opportunities it has to connect with current and potential customers.
- It enables businesses to expand their reach and strengthen the company brand.
- It increases the number of links back to a business' original website.
- It automatically updates when new information is posted.
- Tracking subscribers to RSS feeds is difficult.
- The content of a feed can be copied easily, even without the permission of the business.

Now test yourself

TESTED

1 Explain the difference between static and dynamic web pages.
2 What is the purpose of RSS feeds?
3 How can RSS feeds benefit businesses?
4 How could a photographer use a blog, and what benefits might it have for them?

1.7 Advantages and 1.8 Disadvantages

You must

- understand the advantages and disadvantages of the world wide web to different holders of information.

Type of holder of information	Advantages	Disadvantages
Individuals	Speed of personal communication, e.g. with friends and relatives in other countries	Cyber crime, e.g. identity theft, financial theft
	Easy access to large amounts of information	Cost of internet access, e.g. cost of broadband, cost of equipment (computer, laptop, tablet, mobile phone)
	Access to internet banking and online shopping 24/7	
	Access to music and video	
Organisations	Share large amounts of information quickly, nationally and internationally	Cyber crime, e.g. threats from malicious attacks
	Charities can accept donations 24/7	Cost of developing and maintaining websites and data stores
	Businesses can sell products and services 24/7	
	Businesses can promote their products and services to a wider audience, e.g. globally	

Now test yourself

TESTED

1 Compare the advantages and disadvantages of the world wide web to individuals and organisations.

L01 Understand where information is held globally and how it is transmitted

2.1 Information styles and their uses

You must

- know about the different **information styles**
- understand how different information styles are used for different purposes.

> **Information styles**: the style of the information, regardless of whether technology is used or not; for example, audio could be a recording of a podcast or someone giving a presentation.

Revision activity

Complete the table below to describe how the information styles are used by businesses and individuals.

Information style	Definition	Used for
Text	A human-readable sequence of characters; there are different character sets for different languages	
Graphic	A clear and effective picture and/or illustration	Logos Diagrams Maps Photographs
Video	A recording of moving visual images	Used to earn money (downloading of films, selling sponsorship) Visual instructions – how to do something Demonstrations – show how something works Marketing products Marketing services Promotional videos on websites (who they are and what they do, to advertise a sale or special event) Virtual tours To encourage regular visits to a business' website To stand out from the competition
Animated graphic	Graphics developed to give the illusion of movement	
Audio	Sound within the acoustic range available to humans	Think of sound with video, podcasts, video conferencing – how would businesses and individuals use them?

Information style	Definition	Used for
Numerical	Information that is measurable, e.g. profit and loss, sales, date, time	
Braille	A system of writing and printing for blind or partially sighted people; raised dots are used to represent letters and numbers that can be identified by touch	Used in all forms of documents Used to add text to tactile images, e.g. maps
Tactile images	Raised interpretations of visual images or objects designed to be read by touch, often in conjunction with a detailed description and braille labelling	Used in medical diagnostics Helps businesses to create an inclusive society, e.g. to enable blind or partially sighted people to use maps, explore space, etc.
Subtitles		
Boolean	A binary variable that can have one of two possible values, e.g. yes/no, Y/N, true/false, T/F	
Tables and spreadsheets	Structures that organises information into rows and columns	Databases – used to store and search records for the presentation of related information Spreadsheets – used for the manipulation, calculation and presentation of numerical information
Charts and graphs	Visual representations of numerical information	Identifying trends Making comparisons Analysing sales, profit/loss

Now test yourself

TESTED ☐

1 Explain the purpose of tactile images using a well-constructed example to aid your explanation.
2 A business wants to present their annual sales results to its stakeholders. Which information style should they use? Justify your answer.
3 A health club wants to include demonstrations on how to carry out certain exercises on its website. Which information style could they use (there may be more than one)? Justify your answer.

> **Stakeholder:** a person with an interest or concern in something, a person and/or a business.

2.2 Information classification

You must

- know about different classifications of information
- understand the impact of different classifications of information on the holders of information.

Sensitive

- Data that must be protected from unauthorised access to maintain the privacy and/or security of an individual or organisation.
- There are three main types of sensitive information:
  - **personal** information – personally identifiable information that can be traced back to an individual; any disclosure of this information could have a negative impact on this person, for example identity theft
  - **business** information – information that poses a risk to a business if obtained by a competitor or the general public, for example trade secrets or financial data
  - **classified** information – belonging to a government body and restricted according to level of sensitivity, for example restricted, confidential, secret or top secret; unauthorised access can result in a breach of national security.
- Holders of sensitive information must comply with current regulations and legislation. Failure to comply can result in heavy fines, imprisonment, loss of business and/or reputation.

Private

See personal information above.

Public

- Information that can be made available to the general public.
- It is considered to be desirable and non-objectional by the person/organisation releasing the information.

Personal

- Information recorded about an individual that may or may not be sensitive.

Business

- This can include sensitive and non-sensitive information.
- It can include information on products and/or services, company and executive profiles, credit and financial information, market research, and so on.

Confidential

- Information that is meant to be kept secret or private.
- Examples include new product designs, marketing strategies, software coding, sealed bids when tendering for contracts, recorded discussion between doctor and patient.

Classified

- Information that is deemed sensitive and therefore has restricted access, for example military intelligence.

Impact on holders of information

Holders of information are governed by regulation and legislation. Systems and procedures may need to be put in place in order to adhere to any regulation/legislation, which can be costly for many businesses. Failure to comply can result in:

- heavy fines
- imprisonment
- loss of revenue
- loss of reputation
- loss of productivity
- loss of custom.

Remember

Make sure you know the difference between information style and information classification. It is an easy way to lose marks in an exam.

- **Information style** – how the information is presented, for example text, video, graphic.
- **Information classification** – the sorting of information into different information types, for example sensitive, classified, personal.

Now test yourself　　　　　　　　　　　TESTED ☐

1　Identify the different types of sensitive information that could be held by an organisation. Consider organisational information as well as information relating to individuals.
2　What are the risks to individuals and organisations if this sensitive information is not held securely?
3　Explain the difference between classified and confidential information.
4　Give an example of classified information and an example of confidential information.

2.3 Quality of information

You must

- know about the characteristics of information
- understand why it is important that holders of information have access to good-quality information
- understand the impact of using poor-quality information.

Characteristics

Good information has value and is relevant to the purpose it is being used for. It needs to be accurate, up to date, reliable, comparable, complete and relevant.

Importance of good information

Good information:
- can transform the way business works
- aids decision making
- helps innovation
- helps to mitigate business risks.

Consequences of poor information

The use of poor-quality information can lead to:
- misinformation
- loss of reputation
- loss of finance
- lack of response to potential risks to business.

Now test yourself

TESTED

1 Explain why is it important for businesses to have access to good information.
2 Explain the consequences to a business of using poor information.
3 Identify the characteristics of good information.

You must

- know the steps involved in the management of information
- understand how the management of information can impact on holders in different ways.

Steps involved in the management of information

- **Collecting, storing, retrieving** – for example, adding new records, searching and displaying information.
- **Manipulating and processing** – for example, calculation of numerical data and production of a graph to display the results.
- **Analysing** – for example, looking at patterns to identify trends in sales.
- **Securing** – making sure that stored information is secure and safe, for example by encrypting information prior transmission.
- **Transmitting** – sending information in some format or another to someone else, for example as an attachment via email, via an online collaboration application or uploading on to a website.

Impact on individuals and organisations

- Cost of equipment (including cost of broadband).
- Additional costs to ensure secure storage, for example the purchase of antivirus and **anti-malware** software.
- Compliance with current legislation and regulation – ensuring that the requirements for the secure storage of information are met at all times, and the costs to individuals and organisations are kept to a minimum if security is breached, for example financial penalties.

> **Anti-malware**: software designed to prevent, detect and eradicate malicious software, such as a virus or a worm.

Now test yourself

TESTED

1 Identify the steps involved in the management of information.
2 Discuss the impact of complying with current legislation and regulations to businesses when managing information.

LO3 Understand the use of global information and the benefits to individuals and organisations

3.1 Data versus information

You must

- know the difference between data and information.

- **Data** – raw, unorganised facts that requires processing.
- **Information** – data that has been processed, organised and structured into a meaningful context.

3.2 Categories of information used by individuals

You must

- know about the categories of information
- know how the information can be used by individuals.

Categories of information

- **Communication** – for example emails, messaging, social media, word-processed letters, completing online forms; used to share or exchange ideas, news and information with others.
- **Education and training** – for example researching information online for a project, watching online tutorials, listening to podcasts to obtain information, watching videos on how to do something.
- **Entertainment** – for example reading ebooks, reading product reviews, reading music and film reviews.
- **Planning** – for example using an electronic diary, using online collaboration applications to share resources and information for a collaborative project.
- **Financial** – for example online banking to look at your balance or review spending.
- **Research** – for example to find information about a product or service; looking up recipes, games, films, music; to find information about something to support study on a subject.
- **Location dependent** – for example where to find a specific retail outlet or the telephone number of a local dentist, doctor or optician.

Benefits and limitations

- The internet has a vast amount of information, but it is important that the validity is checked as it may be out of date and/or inaccurate.
- Is internet access readily available? If not, many of the categories cannot be accessed online.
- Online resources are portable and, therefore, can be accessed anywhere where internet access is readily available.
- Many online information sources are free.
- Searching for information can be time-consuming.
- People with visual impairments may struggle to read from computer screens.

Now test yourself

TESTED ☐

1 Explain the difference between data and information.
2 Describe the different categories of information used by individuals.

3.3 Categories of information used by organisations

You must

- know about the categories of information
- know how the information can be used by organisations.

- **Knowledge management and creation** – used to share knowledge within the organisation and to aid the creation of new ideas and 'new knowledge', for example analysing market trends and collaborating on new ideas to increase market share.
- **MIS** – a computer-based system providing an organisation with the tools to organise, manage and evaluate departments within an organisation, for example monitoring staff training, personnel records of all employees and location of staff.
- **Marketing, promotion and sales** – used to identify trends in order to market products and/or services, promote products and/or services and increase sales.
- **Financial analysis and modelling** – used to analyse financial information and build models of real-world financial situations, for example cash-flow forecasts.
- **Contact management** – provides quick access to account names and contact information. Often used with calendaring, email integration and activity management. It is used by individuals or small teams.
- **Decision making** – information is required before an organisation can make a business decision, for example how many extra staff will be required over the Christmas period to deliver products to the customers, how much aid is required by a charity to support a crisis situation in another country.
- **Internal and external communication** – for example, information about new products to be provided to the sales team, notifying a customer that payment is due.
- **Big data** – this is any data that is too large or too complex for traditional data analysis techniques to be used. For example, using social media data, browser logs and sensor data to gain a better understanding of customers and their behaviours, health care organisations can analyse large quantities of structured and unstructured data so that they can provide better diagnoses or treatment options for their patients.

Now test yourself

TESTED

1. Explain the term 'knowledge management and creation'.
2. Identify an example of how a manufacturing company would use knowledge management and creation.
3. Provide a definition for 'big data'.
4. How would a management information system (MIS) be used in a school environment?

3.4 Stages of data analysis

You must

- know about the different stages of data analysis.

- **Identify the need** – what information do you need, what do you need to find out?
- **Define the scope** – how much detail, the content, timescales, constraints, and so on.
- **Identify potential sources** – where are you going to get the information from?
- **Source and select information** – find sources of information and make sure that the information you select is good information.
- **Select the most appropriate tools** – what do you need in order to process, manipulate and present the information?
- **Process and analyse data** – import/input the information and prepare it for analysis, for example processing sales data to produce charts that indicate trends in sales.
- **Record and store information** – save the information and present it in the desired format, for example as a report incorporating charts and graphs.
- **Share results** – for example, email copies of the report to relevant stakeholders.

Now test yourself

1. Draw a flow chart of the different stages of data analysis.
2. Annotate your flow chart with a brief explanation for each of the stages.

You must

- know about the different data analysis tools
- understand the use of them for different contexts
- be able to justify why you would select certain data analysis tools for different contexts.

- **Data tables** – used for databases, for example to store customer records.
- **Visualisation of data** – using graphs and charts, for example to show the number of parking tickets issued over a 12-month period.
- **Trend and pattern identification** – for example, using graphs to show the trend in sales over a set period.
- **Data cleaning** (also known as data cleansing) – the detection and removal of errors, inconsistencies and redundant data to improve the quality of the data, for example removing customers who no longer buy the organisation's products and/or services.
- **Geographic information system, location mapping** – used to capture, store, manipulate, analyse, manage and present all types of geographical data, for example to map changes in a specific geographic area to identify future conditions (such as tsunami alerts) and decide on the course of action to take.

Now test yourself

TESTED

1 You have been provided with a data file from a client containing data that you need to import into a database. The client explains that there is some very old data in the file and that it also contains data relating to products they no longer sell.

What data analysis tool would you use to ensure that the data you import is accurate and up to date? Justify your answer.

2 Provide a description for the term 'data analysis tool'.

Remember
It is important that you understand what is meant by the term 'data analysis tool', what it is and how it is used.

You must

- know about the structure of information systems and their characteristics
- understand the benefits and limitations of each system structure.

Information system structure	Characteristics	Benefits	Limitations
Open system	Allows for free exchange of information between departments and the external environment (outside of the organisation), e.g. marketing departments require external data to inform their marketing strategy Inputs from within the organisation and from external sources Outputs will be provided for internal and external environments	More flexible than a closed environment Can result in shorter development times or the marketing of new products as there are more people to share ideas and collaborate with Can result in more effective problem solving as external factors are taken into consideration Improves communication between organisation and their customers and suppliers	Reliability of data and/or information coming from external sources and/or other departments Open to security risks, e.g. cyber crime
Closed system	Very little sharing internally within an organisation and minimal, if any, interaction with the external environment Each system performs functions for its own area without communicating the activities to other areas within the department	Useful if an organisation is developing a new product idea or concept Protects organisational secrets and prevents leakage of information to competitors More secure to external risks than an open system	Very little flexibility, i.e. not easy to change the structure with changing needs

Now test yourself

TESTED

1 Compare and contrast open and closed information system structures.
2 Explain the benefits of each type of information system structure.

LO4 Understand the legal and regulatory framework governing the storage and use of global information

4.1 UK legislation and regulation relating to the storage and use of information

You must

- know about the legislation and regulations that relate to the storage and use of information
- understand the impact and consequences of legislation and regulations on holders of information.

- **Consequences** – this is not only about what happens to a holder of information if they breach the legislation and regulations, but also what policies they must put in place in order to adhere to them. These consequences can have an impact on an information holder.
- **Impact** – how the legislation and regulations influence what holders do with information and how they store it; the outcome from a breach of regulation/legislation.

Revision activity

Complete the following table making sure that you use the most current UK legislation and regulations.

Current UK legislation/ regulation	Purpose	Impact	Consequences

Now test yourself

TESTED ☐

Refer to the table above, which you have completed, to answer the following questions.
1 What is each piece of legislation/regulation for?
2 What happens to a holder of information if they do not comply with the legislation/regulation?
3 What must a holder of information do/put in place to adhere to the legislation/regulation?

4.2 Global information protection legislation and regulation

You must

- be able to compare and contrast the data protection legislation and regulations in different countries

Revision activity

Complete the following table to identify the different legislation/regulation for different countries (including the UK). Explain the purpose of each and then describe the similarities and differences.

Legislation/regulation	Country/continent	Purpose	Similarities	Differences
	UK			
	Europe			
	North America			
	Asia			
	Africa			
	Australia			

Now test yourself

1 Discuss the similarities and differences between data protection legislation in Europe and Africa.

L04 Understand the legal and regulatory framework governing the storage and use of global information

You must

● know about the global requirements for green IT
● understand the rationale for green IT and the global benefits.

Green IT is a collection of strategic and tactical initiatives to directly reduce the carbon footprint of an individual's or organisation's computing operation. It is not just about reducing the impact of the ICT industry on the environment, but also how ICT can be used to reduce an individual's or organisation's overall carbon footprint. For example, remote working for office workers can reduce the amount of carbon emissions caused by travelling to and from work in a car.

> **Green IT:** the practice of reducing energy consumption from IT equipment and thereby improving sustainability.

Global requirements on organisations and individuals

● **United Nations Climate Change Summits** – at the one in December 2015, the majority of countries in the world adopted the Paris Agreement, committing to work to limit global temperature rise to well below 3° C and to strive for 1.5° C. During each summit, progress is reviewed and further action to address climate change is discussed and agreed.
● **Greening Government: ICT Strategy** – this strategy sets out how the UK government's ICT will contribute to green commitments. The vision is to have a 'cost-effective and energy-efficient ICT estate, which is fully exploited, with reduced environmental impacts to enable new and sustainable ways of working for the public sector'.
● **Global requirements** – for countries to actively reduce their carbon footprint, not only by reviewing their use of ICT but also by using ICT to support the implementation of systems and procedures to support the reduction. It is linked to the United Nations Climate Change Summits.

Carbon footprint

● ICT is responsible for two per cent of global emissions of CO_2, which is similar to that of the aviation industry. A carbon footprint is the CO_2 emissions (greenhouse gas emissions) caused by an individual, event, organisation or product.

Purpose

- Reduce carbon emissions.
- Sustainability, for example to retain global warming at a level of 1.5° C.
- Greater efficiency.
- Save money and time.
- Reduce energy consumption.

Benefits

- Economic – cutting costs, for example energy consumption, transportation, water, waste, disposal, paper.
- Access to potential grants and incentives for implementing green IT.
- Enhancing brand image, for example promoting the fact that the business is dedicated to green initiatives.

Figure 2.3 **Green IT**

Now test yourself

TESTED

1 What is meant by the term 'green IT'?
2 Explain the global requirements for green IT.
3 How can IT help reduce CO_2 emissions?

LO5 Understand the process flow of information

5.1 Information sources and data types

You must

- know about different information sources and data types
- understand when to use different information sources and data types
- be able to justify when to use different information sources and data types within a given context.

Information sources

Internal sources are those from within an organisation, for example:
- financial – relating to performance, profit and loss of the business. Includes cost of purchases, wages, taxes, rates and other overheads
- personnel – information held by the business relating to employees
- marketing – for example, which products and/or services are most successful
- purchasing – types of products and/or services, supplier details, costs of purchases
- sales – for example, current sale price of products and/or services, level of sales
- manufacturing – for example, cost of manufacturing products, cost of raw materials and running machinery, wages for production staff, transportation costs, disposal of waste
- administration – for example, personnel information, communications with internal and external sources, storing of customer and/or supplier information.

External sources are those from outside the organisation, for example:
- supplier price lists
- financial information from a third party
- survey results.

Data types

- **Primary data** – data observed or collected directly from source. It has not had any analysis or processing; it is raw data, for example taking measurements or conducting a survey.
- **Secondary data** – data collected by a third party and available from other sources, for example survey results from a market research company.
- **Qualitative data** – data that is not numeric and can be arranged into categories, for example gender, colours, names, and so on.
- **Quantitative data** – data that can be measured by numbers and can be classified as numerical or continuous, for example the number of products available, the number of employees, the cost of production, and so on.

Now test yourself   TESTED ☐

1 Explain the difference between qualitative and quantitative data, giving well-constructed examples.
2 An online retailer wants to gather feedback on its customer service. What type of data should they collect? Justify your choices.
3 The same online retailer is reviewing the popularity of a variety of products that they sell. It has been decided that it can use internal data sources as well as external data sources. Discuss why both sources would be appropriate.

5.2 Data flow diagrams (DFDs)

You must

- know about level 0 and level 1 DFDs, but you will not be expected to draw DFDs
- understand the components of a DFD and how they are used to show the flow of information
- understand the impacts affecting the flow of information in information systems.

Level 0 DFDs are sometimes called context diagrams. They show little detail but enable the user to gain an overview of how information flows through the system.

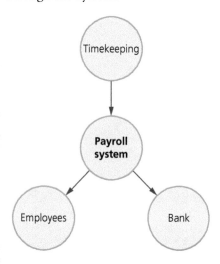

Figure 2.4 DFD with entities and flows (high level)

Level 1 DFDs show how the main processes are broken down into sub-processes.

DFD rules and tips

- Each process should have at least one input and one output.
- Each data store should have at least one data flow in and one data flow out.
- Data stored in a system must go through a process.
- All processes in a DFD must go to another process or data store.
- Each external entity must have at least one input or one output.
- Data flows in one direction.
- Each data flow connects to at least one process.

Entities are external objects outside of the system that the system communicates with. They are sources and destinations of the system's input and outputs, that is, the initiators of data flowing into the business and end recipients of information flowing from the business. For example:

- customer places an order via an e-commerce website (external entity – an initiator of data)
- order is processed, and the customer is notified that the delivery is on its way (external entity – end recipient).

A **process** is anything that changes the data and produces an output. Processes represent the functionalities of the system. A process can only exist once on a DFD.

Data stores represent stored data or control at rest. They are used when different processes need to share information but are active at different times. Information can be written to a store and read from a store.

Many industry **standard symbols** can be used when creating DFDs. The symbols used most commonly are shown in the table below.

Symbol	Purpose
	External entity
	Process
	Data flow
	Data store

Impacts affecting the flow of information in information systems

- Complete or partial system failure – delay in the flow of data.
- Human error – data being lost, misfiled, processed incorrectly.
- Breakdown in working relationships and/or communication – delay in flow of data, delay in processing, delay in storage.

Now test yourself
TESTED

1 What is the difference between a level 0 DFD and a level 1 DFD?
2 What must each external entity in a DFD have?
3 How many directions can the data flow in?
4 Describe the impacts that can affect the flow of information in information systems.
5 Explain what is meant by the term 'entity'.

6.1 Principles of information security

- **Confidentiality** – information can only be accessed by authorised individuals, groups or processes; for example, only people who work in the payroll department and/or human resources department can access information relating to employee's wages.
- **Integrity** – information is maintained to ensure that it is good information, for example accurate, up to date, complete and fit for purpose; for example, the sales figures of a business are kept up to date and accurate so that managers can gather an overview of the business' performance.
- **Availability** – information is available to be used by individuals, groups and processes as and when required; for example, customers of an online shopping company need access to product information so that they can make purchases 24/7.

> **You must**
>
> - know about the aims of information security for holders of information.

Now test yourself

TESTED

1 Describe the aims of information security for holders of information.

6.2 Risks

- **Unauthorised or unintended access to data** –any time when data is accessed by people, organisations or states who have no legal right to access the data. Reasons for unauthorised access include poor security systems and espionage.
- **Accidental loss of data** – the loss of the actual data itself. This can be through human error (someone accidently deleting a file or document) or equipment failure, for example a failing hard drive.
- **Intentional destruction of data** – usually motivated by the desire to have a negative impact on the individual, organisation or state concerned, for example the introduction of viruses that can delete data. Another example is the destruction of data from an old hard drive or system through magnetic wiping; there is always a risk that not all of the data stored on the system has been retrieved prior to destruction.
- **Intentional tampering with data** – the data is still available but it has been tampered with, making it unreliable, for example a disgruntled former employee changing data in revenge for being made redundant.

> **You must**
>
> - understand the risks of breaches in information security.

> **Remember**
>
> Refer to Section 2.1 of Unit 3, which also covers threats to cyber security

Now test yourself

TESTED

1 An organisation is reviewing the security of the information stored on its computer network. Discuss the risks involved of breaches in information security.

> ## You must
>
> - understand the impact of security breaches on holders of information.

- **Loss of intellectual property** – creations of the mind, inventions, literary and artistic work, symbols, names and images used in commerce.
  - ○ **Industrial property** – includes patents for inventions, trademarks, industrial designs and geographical indications.
  - ○ **Copyright** – includes literary and artistic works, for example novels, poems, plays, films, music, drawings, paintings, photographs, sculptures and architectural design.
- **Loss of service and access** – for example, denial of service (DoS) attacks resulting in a system or network resource becoming unavailable to the intended users, or a botnet attack resulting in a network, network device, website or IT environment being taken down.
- **Failure in security of confidential information** – confidential and/or sensitive information could be accessed by unauthorised people.
- **Loss of information belonging to a third party** – for example, cloud storage providers store data and information for third parties (that is, other businesses); if they have a breach in security the data and information held for third parties could be lost. Another example could be the loss of customer details held by a business or information relating to the employees of a business.
- **Loss of reputation** – public opinion of the business will be negative and can result in the business losing money. For example, Yahoo confirmed that all of its 3 billion users were likely compromised in 2013 due to a breach that was not disclosed until mid-2016.
- **Threat to national security** – a threat to the security and safety of a nation state including its citizens, economies and institutions. For example, attacks on IT systems to obtain information relating to military availability, deployment, and so on.

Research recent cases of failures of information security based on the categories above and complete the table below.

Example of failure	How did it occur?	Impact on organisation/state	How was it resolved?

Now test yourself

TESTED

1   A car manufacturer has had a breach in the security of its computer systems. Explain the different impacts this could have on the company.

You must

- know about the different protection measures to mitigate breaches in information security
- understand how the different measures can be used
- be able to justify the use of different protection methods within a given context.

Protection measures

Organisations should have **policies** in place to help mitigate the risks of security breaches, for example:

- **access rights to information**, for example who is allowed access to what information
- **staff responsibilities for maintaining the security of information**, for example logging out of a system when away from your desk, not sharing usernames and passwords with others
- **disaster recovery** – creating an IT disaster recovery plan to implement in the event of a security breach; this is a documented procedure that should be followed to recover and protect a business' IT infrastructure
- **information security risk assessments**, for example to continually monitor the IT infrastructure of a business in order to discover, correct and prevent security problems
- **evaluation of the effectiveness of protection measures**, for example to review the effectiveness of the protection measures implemented by a business to ensure that they are fit for purpose
- **training of staff to handle information**, for example not divulging information to unauthorised people, logging out of IT systems when not at desks, ensuring unauthorised people cannot see the computer screen.

Physical protection

Physical protection refers to the protection of locations and equipment (and all information and software contained therein) from theft, vandalism, natural disasters, man-made catastrophes and accidental damage. It may include:

- **using locks, keypads and biometrics** (facial, retinal or voice recognition) to access workstations, the server room and even buildings themselves
- **placing computers above known flood levels**, for example on the top floors of buildings
- **backing up systems to other locations**, for example backing up data and systems and storing the backups in any other location but the location where the data and system information can usually be found. Backing up on to cloud storage is another option, as well as storing it on a different site.
- **security staff** – to monitor buildings and prevent unauthorised access
- **shredding old paper-based records** – many organisations and individuals use cross-shred shredders as it is almost impossible to 'rebuild' the shredded paper. There are businesses that, for a fee, will take paper-based records and shred them securely. Individuals are advised to shred paper information that includes personal details, such as their name and address, rather than throwing them in the bin where they can be retrieved by criminals.

Figure 2.5 Physical protection: iris recognition

Logical protection

Logical protection refers to technology-based methods used to prevent illegal access to information and systems, such as:

- **tiered levels of access** – different people within an organisation will require different access levels to computer systems and associated information; for example, the sales department would not require access to the payroll system and, therefore, would not have the relevant access level
- **firewalls** – a protective system that lies between the computer network and the internet; an ideal firewall configuration will comprise both software and hardware firewalls:
  - ○ **software firewall** – a piece of software installed on to a computer; it allows some control over its function and features but will only protect the computer it is installed on, not the network
  - ○ **hardware firewall** – built into a router or a stand-alone device; it provides greater protection than a software-based firewall and is easier to administer
- **anti-malware applications** – a type of software program developed to prevent, detect and quarantine any malicious programming on individual computer devices and IT systems
- **obfuscation** – the practice of making something difficult to understand; programming code and data is coded so that it is difficult for an unauthorised person to read it
- **encryption of data at rest** – protecting data that is not moving through networks, for example data stored on a hard drive, laptop or flash drive; the data is converted into a code so that it cannot be easily read
- **encryption of data in transit** – protecting data that is moving from one location to another, for example across the internet or through a private network; as well as the security measures already mentioned, data is also encrypted, that is, converted into code as with data at rest
- **password protection** – only people with authorised passwords can gain access to certain information; passwords should be:
  - ○ strong (a combination of numbers, letters and symbols)
  - ○ not easily guessed, so, not 123456
  - ○ changed regularly.

> **Data at rest:** data stored on a laptop, hard drive, flash drive or archived.
>
> **Data in transit:** data actively moving from one location to another via the internet or across a private network.

1.1 Cyber security aims to protect information

REVISED

You must

- know what is meant by the term 'cyber security'
- know about digital systems
- understand why the information stored on digital systems needs to be kept secure at all times.

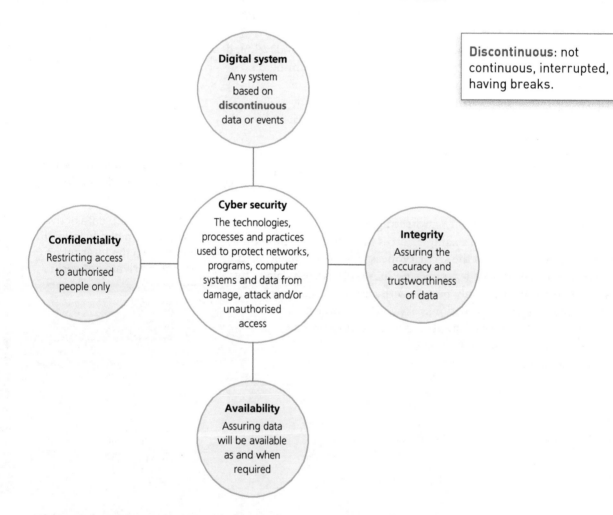

Discontinuous: not continuous, interrupted, having breaks.

Figure 3.1 The relationship between cyber security, digital systems and information

Information must be kept secure to:

- comply with current legislation, for example the General Data Protection Regulation (GDPR) and the Computer Misuse Act (1990)
- protect a company's assets, for example financial information and intellectual property, and to prevent the publishing of sensitive data
- protect individuals from crime, for example identity fraud, bullying and financial loss
- protect government information, for example security plans, defence plans, weapons specifications and financial information.

Now test yourself

TESTED

1 Provide a definition for the term 'cyber security'.
2 What is a digital system?
3 Explain why information must be kept secure.

1.2 Types of cyber security incidents

You must

- know the types and nature of cyber security incidents
- understand how they affect individuals, states and organisations.

Types of cyber security incidents include:
- **Unauthorised access** – gaining access to computer systems, networks, programs and data without permission
  - ○ **hacking** – illegally using a computer to access information stored on another computer system or to spread a virus
  - ○ **escalation of privileges** – obtaining the rights to access and edit information that normal users do not normally have
    - – **vertical** – finding flaws in the security system or operating system to increase their level of access (used to access Androids and IOS smartphones in particular), for example trying to access the system as a teacher when you are a student
    - – **horizontal** – gaining access to other users' areas by stealing their username and password, or due to a program fault that provides a view of data belonging to others.
- **Information disclosure** – information passed to a person, organisation or state without the permission of the owner.
- **Modification of data** – data that is entered, amended, stored or deleted without authorisation (can be accidental).
- **Inaccessible data** – data that is not available to those with authorisation; it can be due to:
  - ○ **account lockout** – the account is locked due to failed login attempts
  - ○ **denial of service (DoS)** – an attack to shut down a computer system, network or website, making it inaccessible.
- **Destruction** – permanent deletion of data through:
  - ○ **malware** – software including viruses, worms, Trojan horses and spyware; used to steal, encrypt or delete sensitive data, alter or hijack computing functions or monitor users' computer activity
  - ○ **deliberate erasure** – data deleted from a computer system on purpose and without permission to cause problems for individuals, organisations and states.
- **Theft** – stealing computer-based information from an unknown victim with the intent of compromising privacy or obtaining confidential information.

> **Malware:** software designed to cause disruption or damage to data and/or a computer system/network.

Now test yourself

1 Define the term 'hacking'.
2 Explain what is meant by 'unauthorised access through the escalation of privileges'.
3 Describe how data can become inaccessible.
4 Destruction is the permanent deletion of data. Explain how this can occur.

1.3 The importance of cyber security

You must

● know why cyber security is important.

Cyber security is important to protect:
● personal data (for example financial data, identity)
● an organisation's data (for example intellectual property, financial data, research on new products prior to launch)
● a state's data (for example national security, economic plans, financial data).

Now test yourself

TESTED

1 Identify what cyber security protects.
2 Describe why it is important to have cyber security in place.

LO2 Understand the issues surrounding cyber security

2.1 Threats to cyber security

You must

- know the wide range of threats to cyber security, whether they are deliberate or accidental.

- **Vulnerabilities** – any weakness within a computer system, network and/or procedures that leaves the security of information exposed to a threat from a cyber attack, including:
  - ○ **system attacks** – for example DoS, botnet, social engineering
  - ○ **physical** – for example theft of portable equipment such as laptops, tablets and portable drives
  - ○ **environmental** – for example floods, fire and earthquakes.
- **Accidental** – unintentional events, for example spilling liquid on a computer, responding to a phishing email, accidental uploading of malware, accidental deletion of data.
- **Intentional** – criminal activities intent on harming computer systems, for example hacking, social engineering, DoS, botnet.
- **Organised** crime:
  - ○ **cyber-enabled crime** – for example fraud, theft and bullying using IT
  - ○ **cyber-dependent crime** – crime that can only be carried out using computer networks and systems, for example spreading malware, hacking and DoS.
- **State-sponsored** – countries spying on each other to obtain information such as on military campaigns, nuclear facilities and government policies, and to spread fake news.

> **Cyber enabled**: illegal activities that can be undertaken without the use of computers.
>
> **Cyber dependent**: illegal activities that depend on the use of computers and the internet.

Now test yourself

TESTED

1 What is the difference between cyber-enabled crime and cyber-dependent crime?
2 You have been asked to review a computer network system for an organisation. Describe the vulnerabilities you would be considering.
3 What is state-sponsored cyber crime?

2.2 Types of attackers and 2.3 Motivation for attackers

REVISED ☐

You must

● know the types of attacker including their characteristics and their motivations.

Type of attacker	Activity	Motivation	Characteristics
Hacktivist	Illegal access to a computer system or network	Politically or socially motivated – they disagree with someone else's viewpoint	Activities are disruptive as opposed to destructive Can be state sponsored Can be IT professionals Can be disaffected young people
Cyber criminal	Uses computers to perform malicious activities, e.g. identity and data theft, spreading viruses Uses computers as a weapon for sending spam or committing fraud Uses computers as an accessory to save stolen or illegal data	Financial gain Espionage Create havoc	Often works in organised groups Sells services to the highest bidder Includes programmers, IT experts, hackers, fraudsters, system hosts and providers, cashiers, money mules, tellers
Insider	A threat from within an organisation, e.g. an employee, former employee, temporary worker or customer Threats can be malicious or accidental	Personal use Financial gain Sabotage, e.g. for revenge, to settle a score	Tends to violate organisational rules and regulations Lack of self-control Antisocial behaviour Desires revenge
Script kiddie	Uses existing computer scripts or code to hack into computers and deface websites	Wants the power of a hacker without the training involved Thrill of hacking Publicity	Teenagers Will over-emphasise their computer abilities Steals code claiming it as their own Little or no hacking skills
Vulnerability broker	Find bugs in programs and systems of other companies; may sell the information to others or to the companies concerned	Financial gain	May have formerly been a cyber criminal A high level of IT expertise with respect to programs and systems
Scammers (cyber enabled)	Offer goods or opportunities to others to make 'quick money' by sending emails with a false link Targets many people at one time	Financial gain Identity fraud (to sell to others or use themselves)	Likable and confident personality Will not answer questions about themselves May ask for money using a hard luck story

→

Type of attacker	Activity	Motivation	Characteristics
Phishers (cyber dependent)	Obtains sensitive information for malicious intent, e.g. obtaining credit card details to steal money by redirecting the person to a false website Targets individuals	Financial gain Theft of intellectual property	Can be from anywhere in the world but common areas are Middle East and Asia, as well as the USA; Eastern Europe is notable for money scams
Cyber terrorists	Uses computers and communication systems to cause fear or intimidation in a society through the destruction of or damage to people, property and systems	To instil fear in others To intimidate a society into changing for the purpose of an ideological goal Righting perceived wrongs	Can be based anywhere in the world May have ideological or religious reasons for wanting to terrorise others Personal gain High-end programming skills

Now test yourself

TESTED

1 A hacker is an individual using computer, networking and other skills to overcome a technical problem. The term tends to refer to a person who uses their skills to gain unauthorised access to computer systems and networks in order to commit crimes, for example to steal information for identity theft, damage or to bring down systems and hold organisations to ransom for monetary gain. There are three types of hacker: white hat, black hat and grey hat. Research each of these types of hackers and provide a description of each.
2 Describe the motivation for a script kiddie to hack into a computer system.
3 What are the characteristics of a hacktivist and their motivation for carrying out cyber crime?
4 What is a vulnerability broker?

Remember
If you are asked to identify different cyber attackers in an exam paper, do not just use the term hacker. The examiner wants you to talk about the different types, for example phisher or script kiddie.

2.4 Targets for cyber security threats

You must

- know the different targets for cyber security threats
- know how the threats may manifest themselves.

- People via:
  - internet shopping, for example fake websites, unauthorised cookies, weak passwords
  - emails
  - social media, for example information, photographs and/or videos providing cyber criminals with information about an individual and/or their family.
- Organisations (public, private, third party/not for profit) via:
  - internal/external hacking
  - DoS (denial of service)
  - botnet
  - theft of equipment
  - theft of data
  - data misuse
  - computer misuse.
- Equipment – particularly mobile devices – can be:
  - stolen
  - left unattended
  - used in unsecure areas with unsecure network access
  - lost, for example left in a taxi or on a train
  - inadvertently infected with malware via email or the downloading of software and/or apps.

All of this results in the theft of information, whether it is about an individual, an organisation or a state/country.

Revision activity

Complete the table below to identify how the different security threats can occur.

Target	Activity	Type of attack						
		Hacking	DoS	Botnet	Theft of equipment	Theft of data	Data misuse	Computer misuse
People	Internet shopping and general internet use							
People	Social media							
People	Email							
Public organisation								
Private organisation								
Not-for-profit organisation								

2.5 Impacts of cyber security incidents

You must

- know the possible impacts of cyber security incidents
- understand how these affect different stakeholders in a variety of different ways.

Impacts:

- global problem for individuals, organisations and states
- loss of confidentiality, integrity, availability, data, finance, business, identity, reputation and customer confidence
- disruption of people's lives, business, industry, transport, the media and utilities
- safety, for example for oil installations and traffic control.

Revision activity

Complete the table below by researching the incidents listed in the first column and identifying the impact that they had on individuals, organisations and states. Remember that loss is not just a loss of information: it can be a loss of reputation and/or business.

Type of incident	Impact on individuals	Impact on organisations	Impact on states
WannaCry: a global incident			
Yahoo: a loss incident			
DoS attack on the BBC: a disruption incident			

One of the attacks listed above had an impact on safety. Which incident was it? What was the impact (if any) on individuals, organisations and states?

REVISED

You must

- know about the other cyber security considerations
- understand the implications for different stakeholders in the wider context
- be aware of the latest and/or most up-to-date versions of legislation.

Revision activity

The table below contains some examples of other considerations of cyber security. Complete the 'implications for stakeholders' column. Think of other examples and add them to the table.

Ethical (morally right or wrong)	Legal	Operational	Implications for stakeholders
Ethical hacking: • IT specialists • employed or contracted by individuals/ organisations to identify vulnerabilities in their systems/ networks **Organisations** monitoring the activities of employees without their knowledge; agreed as ethical by some but unethical by others **States** 'spying' on each other (see State-sponsored crime in Section 2.1, Unit 3)	Current legislation includes: • Communications Act (2003) • Privacy and Electronic Communications (EC Directive) Regulations 2003 • GDPR (EU) 2016/679 • Computer Misuse Act (1990) • Official Secrets Act (1989)	Security measures that must be implemented in order to mitigate cyber security attacks including: • regular testing of systems and networks for possible vulnerabilities • keeping operating systems and software up to date • monitoring antivirus and anti-malware software • implementing secure remote access methods • using firewalls • using strong passwords • training employees • implementing relevant policies and procedures	

Now test yourself

TESTED

1 Explain the term 'ethical hacking'.
2 Describe two other ethical considerations that need to be considered.
3 Discuss the current legislation that applies to cyber security.

LO3 Understand measures used to protect against cyber security incidents

3.1 Cyber security risk management

You must

- know about the various measures that should be taken to manage cyber security
- understand and be able to justify the implementation of different measures than can be used for a given context.

Identify assets and mitigate risks:

- What are the assets (hardware, software, communications equipment, information and data)?
- What are the risks to these assets (likelihood of a cyber attack being successful or taking place and how it may occur)?

Mitigate risks – testing systems and networks for vulnerabilities.

Monitor and control systems – how assets can be monitored and controlled.

Protect vulnerabilities – measures that can be put in place to protect the assets and how they protect the assets.

Costs/benefits – what are the cost implications and what are the benefits? Do the benefits outweigh the costs?

Now test yourself

1 Describe the different measures taken to manage cyber security.
2 A computer network system has recently been installed. What measures would you consider to protect the network from attack and why? (Think of the measures used to manage cyber security as this will help you with your justification.)

You must

- know about different testing and monitoring measures used to test vulnerabilities
- understand and be able to justify the effectiveness of different measures for a given context.

- **Vulnerability testing** – identification of a list of vulnerabilities that can be prioritised in order of severity.
- **Penetration testing** – where an attack is simulated (it should be requested by the client); it is designed to achieve a specific goal.
- **Fuzzing** – used to identify coding errors and security loopholes in software, operating systems and networks. It involves inputting huge amounts of random data in an attempt to make the system crash.
- **Security functionality** – used to identify flaws in security mechanisms that are supposed to protect data and information and maintain functionality.
- **Sandboxing** – test environment that isolates untested code changes to ensure that any issues are not transmitted to other areas of the system.
- **Intrusion detection system (IDS)** – device or software used to monitor systems for malicious activity.
- **Network intrusion detection system (NIDS)** – monitors all inbound and outbound network activity to identify any suspicious patterns that indicate a cyber security attack.
- **Host intrusion detection system (HIDS)** – firewalls, antivirus software and spyware detection programs installed on every network computer that has two-way access to the external environment, for example internet access. Monitors inbound and outbound packets for the device for any suspicious activity.
- **Distributed intrusion detection system (DIDS)** – consists of multiple IDSs over a large network that communicate with each other or a central server. Provides a broader view of the network activity and facilitates faster analysis of any issues.
- **Anomaly based** – monitors network and system activity and classifies whether the activity is as expected or not.
- **Signature based** – monitors specific patterns for network traffic or known instruction sequences used by malware. It must be kept up to date in order to be effective (as with antivirus and anti-malware software) and require regular signature updates.
- **Honeypot** – a computer system set up as a decoy to detect, deflect and even counteract any unauthorised use of the system.
- **Intrusion prevention system (IPS)** – proactive detection and prevention against unwanted intruders, for example a firewall.

Penetration testing: a software tool that tests a computer system/network to identify vulnerabilities that could be exploited by an attacker.

Fuzzing: a method used to test the security of software.

Intrusion detection system (IDS): software that monitors computer system/network activities for unexpected or malicious activities.

Anomaly based: software designed to detect computer intrusions and misuse by monitoring the activity taking place and classifying whether it is normal or anomalous.

Honeypot: a server or computer system set up as a decoy to gather information on intruders or attackers of computer systems/ networks.

Now test yourself

TESTED

1 Explain the term 'fuzzing' and when it would be used.
2 What is the purpose of sandboxing?
3 Explain the term 'anomaly based'.
4 What is the purpose of a honeypot?

You must

● know about the different security controls and their characteristics
● have an understanding of the different controls for a given context and be able to justify their effectiveness.

Physical

Limits access to buildings, rooms and physical IT assets, for example:

● **biometrics** – a person's physical characteristics can be used for identification and access control
● **swipe cards** – magnetic cards allow authorised people access to buildings, rooms and/or IT systems; can be lost and/or stolen
● **alarms** – located near access points to buildings and rooms alarms do not prevent entry but may deter people due to the risk of being caught.

Hardware

Prevents the physical removal of items, for example:

● **safe** – to securely store small items of equipment such as tablets, phones and removal storage drives, as well as backups of data
● **cable locks** – used to secure items such as laptops and computers to very large, immovable objects, for example a desk
● **engraving** – engraving the details of the owner on the hardware
● **SmartWater** – a non-hazardous liquid that leaves a long-lasting and unique identifier; its presence is invisible except under an ultraviolet light.

Figure 3.2 Cable lock

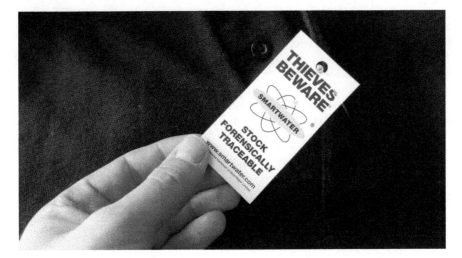

Figure 3.3 SmartWater

Software

Software helps to prevent unauthorised access to networks, computer systems and data:

- **firewall** – controls and monitors incoming and outgoing traffic on a network or system and decides whether to allow or block identified traffic based on the defined security rules
- **anti-malware** – protects a system from malware infiltration and infection
- **operating system updates** – protects against cyber attacks by removing and/or correcting vulnerabilities with the system that have been identified
- **patch management** – the process of updating patches for software and applications to fix any security vulnerabilities; acquiring, testing and installing code changes or patches to software on a computer system/network.

Encryption

Encryption protects the confidentiality of digital data while it is stored or transmitted using the internet or computer networks, as well as when using removable or mobile devices.

- **Asymmetric encryption** – also known as public key cryptography. It uses two keys to encrypt plaintext (unencrypted information). Anything encrypted using a public key can only be decrypted using a private key. It tends to be used in day-to-day communication channels, especially over the internet.
- **Symmetric encryption** – only uses one key shared among the people who need access to the data.

Cryptography

Cryptography protects information and resources on open and closed networks.

Procedures

Access management – the process of granting authorised users access to a computer system, network and associated data, as well as preventing access by unauthorised users.

Data backup – the process of copying and/or archiving data, including files and folders, so that they can be restored should the data be lost from a system.

Remote working – assessing the risks involved with remote and mobile working:

- the type of information and services that can be accessed or stored on devices
- increasing the level of monitoring on all remote connections and the systems being accessed
- users should be trained with respect to:
  ○ secure storage and management of user information
  ○ incident reporting
  ○ social engineering
  ○ shoulder surfing
- all mobile devices should have a secure baseline of security configuration
- the amount of information stored on a mobile device should be kept to the minimum
- data should have some form of encryption.

> **Access management:** managing the access to a computer system and/or network.

Now test yourself

TESTED ☐

1 Explain the term 'cryptography'.
2 An organisation has asked you to explain what remote working procedures they need to implement. You should justify why they are important.
3 What is the difference between asymmetric and symmetric encryption?
4 Discuss the hardware, software and physical controls that can be put in place to help mitigate cyber security attacks.

Remember

You will be presented with a case study prior to your exam and you will need to analyse it carefully. You may need to consider the potential cyber security incidents that may occur and how an organisation and/or individual could:

- manage the risks
- test and monitor the computer systems/networks
- select and implement cyber security controls.

LO4 Understand how to manage cyber security incidents

4.1 Responding to an incident

You must

- know about different procedures that should be followed in the event of a cyber security incident, including conducting investigations or being the subject of an investigation
- understand why certain procedures should be followed in a given context
- be able to justify the procedures followed in a given context.

- **Responsibilities** – who is involved? What are their responsibilities?
- **Who to contact** – who needs to be informed and what do they need to be told?
- **Procedures**:
  - What are they?
  - When do they need to be implemented?
  - What order do they need to be carried out in?
  - Why are they important?
- **Extent of the incident** – what is the impact of the incident? Is it on hardware, software, network or information, or one or more of them?
- **Contain the incident**:
  - isolate certain sensitive systems or data (which is the priority?), devices, hardware and sections of the network
  - implement security measures to detect and mitigate additional incident-related activity.
- **Eradicate the incident**, for example:
  - delete malware
  - disable breached user accounts
  - identify and mitigate vulnerabilities
  - identify all affected hosts.
- **Reduce the impact and recover from the incident**, for example:
  - restore systems to normal operation and confirm they are functioning normally
  - rebuild systems from scratch
  - replace compromised files
  - install patches
  - change passwords
  - develop procedures to reduce the risk of this reoccurring.

Now test yourself

1. When carrying out a cyber security incident investigation, explain why it is important to know:
   - the responsibilities of individuals
   - who to contact.
2. Explain the term 'contain the incident' using a well-constructed example.
3. Describe how you can eradicate the incident.
4. How can an organisation reduce the impact and recover from the incident?

4.2 Cyber security incident report

You must

- know the various stages of investigation that should be undertaken should a cyber security incident occur
- have an understanding and justification for decisions that must be taken in a given context
- be able to complete sections of a cyber security report.

A cyber security report normally includes:

- **Incident title and date of incident** – the exact date is important as it can be cross-referenced with other activity, for example anti-malware software or updating of patches.
- **Target of the incident** – was it the organisation, a particular department or person? Then consider whether the target was the hardware, software, network or information.
- **Incident category**:
  - ○ **critical** – organisation is no longer able to provide some critical services to users, lives may be lost
  - ○ **significant** – loss of reputation, disruption to services, financial loss
  - ○ **minor** – inconvenient, loss of efficiency but able to provide services
  - ○ **negligible** – minimal impact on systems, services and users.
- **Description of the incident**, for example:
  - ○ what problem did it create
  - ○ how was it discovered
  - ○ what type of incident it was.
- **Type of attacker(s)**, for example:
  - ○ internal (for example an employee)
  - ○ external
  - ○ one person, a group or a government.
- **Purpose of incident** – what was the attacker(s) trying to achieve, for example:
  - ○ financial gain
  - ○ political advantage
  - ○ destruction of reputation.
- **Techniques used by attacker(s)** – how did they attack the system?
- **Capability of attacker(s)** – how effective were they?
- **Impact of the incident on business, data, recovery time**

Figure 3.4 **Responding to a cyber security incident**

- **Cost of the incident**, for example:
  - **financial** – loss of money, cost of recovery time, loss of working time
  - **reputation** – has it damaged the reputation of the organisation? If so, how?
- **Responses needed** – who it was reported to (this could include the police, cyber crime units, software developers).
- **Future management**, for example:
  - **review of incident** – what worked and what did not work
  - **evaluation to include identification of trends** – look at the results to identify any trends, failures, omissions, successes
  - **update of documentation, key information, procedures and controls** – to reflect the outcome of the review and evaluation, that is, changes to be made to improve the effectiveness of policies and procedures.
  - **recommendations of changes** – changes to current practice/plans to mitigate further attacks.

Now test yourself

TESTED ☐

1. Describe the different incident categories.
2. Why is it important to have the exact date of the incident in the incident report?
3. Explain the importance of including the cost of the incident in the incident report. Give examples of what the costs may be and the impact these could have on an organisation.

Exam techniques

In an exam it is not just a case of what you know, but how you apply that knowledge under exam conditions. Getting a good grounding in exam techniques is as important as revising. Some of the skills that you will need to work on include:
- following the instructions on the exam paper
- responding appropriately to the command verbs, for example 'identify', 'describe', 'explain', 'discuss', 'justify', 'analyse' and 'evaluate'
- writing your answers using appropriate language, for example using correct technical terminology where required
- using the knowledge you have gained from different parts of the unit specification to answer specific questions (this is especially important when answering questions based on a case study).

Answering multiple-choice questions

Answering multiple-choice questions is different to answering extended-answer exam questions. Some questions will take you longer to answer than others.

Always read the instructions carefully:
- Does it ask you to select one or more possible answers?
- Does it ask for a negative? For example: 'Which **one** of the following is **not** …?'
- Look for keywords given in bold – this gives you a clue as to what is required.
- Read through all of the questions, quickly answering all of the ones you definitely know the answer to and leaving the hardest ones until last.
- Try to think of the answer *before* you look at the choices.
- Attempt *all* multiple-choice questions as you have nothing to lose and everything to gain. Even if you are not sure of the answer, it is still worth a guess.

Answering extended-answer questions

- Always read the instructions carefully – what is the command verb (for example 'identify', 'select', 'state', 'describe', 'explain', 'discuss', 'analyse', 'evaluate', 'justify') asking for?
- Concentrate on one question at a time and ask yourself the following:
  - Do I understand what the question is about?
  - How many marks is the question worth? Always work to one minute per mark and no longer.
  - How many parts are there to the question?
  - Can I provide a well-constructed answer?
  - How am I going to answer the question?
  - Do I need to include one or more examples?
  - Do I need to relate my answer to a particular context, that is, do I need to relate it to the organisation/business/situation within the case study?
  - Do I need to use technical terminology?

- It is important that the person marking your paper can not only read your handwriting but also understand what it is you are trying to tell them. If they cannot read it or understand it, they cannot award you marks.
- If you make a mistake, cross it out neatly and then start again (you can always ask for more paper).
- Read through what you have written carefully and ask yourself:
  - Have I answered the question?
  - Have I answered all parts of the question?
  - Have I met the demands of the command verb, for example have I 'explained'?
  - Have I used the correct technical terminology?

Command verb/key word	Depth	Example
Identify	Tests your skill in remembering information Select from a list of options Give a list	Identify **one** type of operating system. **[1]** An acceptable response would be: *Multiuser* **[1]**
Describe	What is it? You would need to provide a number of points that need to be linked and include the main features	Describe **one** characteristic of an extranet. **[2]** An acceptable response could be: *It is similar to an intranet* **[1]** *and is accessible via a web portal.* **[1]**
Explain	What is the purpose of something, i.e. what does it do? How does something work? You will need to provide an explanation with reasoning If the question has a given context, then your answer must relate to the context	Explain what is meant by the term vulnerability testing. **[4]** An acceptable response could be: *Vulnerability testing is the testing of a computer system, network or software* **[1]** *to identify* **[1]** *and prioritise any vulnerabilities/ weaknesses* **[1]** *that could be open to a cyber attack.* **[1]**
Justify	This is about giving reasons for your answers You will usually be asked to identify something first and then you will justify why you have identified it	Identify a simple network topology for two computers in a small office. Justify your choice of network topology. **[4]** An acceptable response could be: *A peer-to-peer (P2P) network topology could be used for a small office.* **[1]** *A peer-to-peer network does not require a separate server* **[1]** *and it is easier to set up* **[1]** *and costs less.* **[1]**
Discuss	This is about providing a response that explores the issue/situation that is being referred to in the question You need to consider different viewpoints and ideas as well as the strengths/ weaknesses, advantages/disadvantages These are usually 8- to 10-mark questions You would provide your answer in an essay-style format	Discuss how membership of professional bodies can enhance the professionalism of individuals and employers. **[10]** In order to answer this question, you would include things such as: - the purpose of professional bodies - the benefits and limitations to individuals - the benefits and limitations to employers.

→

Command verb/key word	Depth	Example
Analyse	You need to break down the idea or information into its component parts You need to explore each component in order to reach a conclusion You need to provide detailed justifications for the conclusion(s) you have reached	Analyse the system requirements for the client in order to recommend an appropriate network topology. **[10]** You would explore things such as: ● the purpose of the system ● who will use the system ● what will be stored on the system ● what components make up the system ● security requirements for the system ● any system vulnerabilities You would then form your conclusions and justify why you have come to those conclusions.
Evaluate	You are required to provide a reasoned argument taking into account a range of factors You should consider strengths/ weaknesses, advantages/disadvantages You should consider all points of view	Evaluate the effectiveness of the cyber security risk management process implemented by the business. **[10]** You would consider the strengths and weaknesses of the processes and how effective they are. You would indicate what you have based your judgements on.

Levels of response style questions (7+ mark style questions)

To gain the higher marks you need to:
● Read the question carefully and take a moment to think about it.
  ○ What exactly is it asking?
  ○ Are you being asked to argue a point?
  ○ Are you being asked to demonstrate your technical knowledge?
  ○ Is it linked to the case study or does it have its own scenario?
● Provide a well-developed line of reasoning that is clear and logically structured by:
  ○ deciding on your main idea
  ○ thinking about how you can explain your idea
  ○ using a number of well-constructed examples, putting the most important/effective example first to add detail to your explanation.
● Review your answer and ask yourself:
  ○ Have I answered the question?
  ○ Could I add anything more? If the answer is yes, then add more detail, possibly using further examples.
  ○ Have I used the correct technical terminology?

> ### Remember
> - Many of the questions will relate to a business context. The examples and answers you give in the exam must always link back to the business context in the question. You will not be asked about a specific input, output or communication device, but you may be asked to identify relevant devices for a business context. You would need to be able to describe what it is, what it is used for and the benefits and limitations to a business if they use it.
> - Always use the full technical terminology when referring to computer components, for example USB drive or flash drive.
> - When providing explanations, include some well-thought-out examples to show your depth of understanding. An example could be with respect to problem solving. If you were being interviewed for a position as an IT technician for an e-commerce business, it is important that you can tackle problems and be able to solve them. This would be valued by the employer because you would be effective in your job role; if there was a problem with the computer system, you would be able to solve it or find a way of solving it with minimum downtime. Downtime for an e-commerce business can result in a loss of sales and, therefore, a loss of profit.

Pre-released case studies

There are pre-released case studies for Units 2 and 3. You should study them very carefully and highlight the key points from the text. See if you can identify where these key points link to the teaching content within the unit.

At the end of each case study, there are a number of bullet points asking you to conduct further research on specific topics. It is important that you do this thoroughly as you will be asked questions about these topics.

Legislation

You need to know what each of the legislations are for:
- Who and what do they protect?
- What are the **implications for** the different stakeholders, and the **impact on** the different stakeholders if they are not adhered to?

You must also ensure that you know the most current legislation.

So, now it's over to you to revise the subjects and practise your exam techniques. Good luck with your exams!

Glossary of terms

access management: managing the access to a computer system and/or network.

anti-malware: software designed to prevent, detect and eradicate malicious software, such as a virus or a worm.

anomaly based: software designed to detect computer intrusions and misuse by monitoring the activity taking place and classifying whether it is normal or anomalous.

backbone: a large transmission line that carries data gathered from smaller lines that interconnect with it.

biometric access: access to a computer system, network, room or building using technology that analyses human body characteristics for authentication purposes, for example fingerprints, retinas and voice patterns.

botnet: a network system infected with malicious software allowing control without the owner's knowledge or consent.

characteristic: a feature or quality of something that helps to identify it.

change management: the systematic approach to dealing with change from the perspective of an organisation and individuals.

communication device: a hardware device that transmits data from one machine to another using analogue or digital signals.

computer hardware: the physical parts attached to a computer, for example a monitor, mouse or keyboard.

computer components: the internal or built-in elements of a computer system enabling it to run, for example the processor, storage or power supply.

cryptography: protecting data by encrypting it into a format called cipher text.

cyber criminal: someone who commits illegal activities using computers and the internet.

cyber dependent: illegal activities that depend on the use of computers and the internet.

cyber enabled: illegal activities that can be undertaken without the use of computers.

data at rest: data stored on a laptop, hard drive, flash drive or archived.

data in transit: data actively moving from one location to another via the internet or across a private network.

denial of service (DoS): an attempt to disrupt a network and/or organisation by issuing more requests than the system can cope with.

describe: to write about something giving characteristics and qualities.

discontinuous: not continuous, interrupted, having breaks.

discuss: talk about a topic.

encapsulation: the inclusion of one thing within another thing.

encryption: data is converted from a readable format to an encoded version that can only be decoded by another device if it has access to the decryption key.

ethical hacking: an attempt to penetrate a computer system/network on behalf of the owner in order to investigate security vulnerabilities that could allow malicious hackers to exploit it.

ethical issues: used to create a moral and fair environment, to avoid discrimination and to promote a principled work ethic.

explain: leads on from a description to include the purpose or reasons.

firewall: software designed to protect a computer system/network from unauthorised access.

fuzzing: a method used to test the security of software.

geostationary: moves in a circular orbit in the plane of the equator so that it appears stationary in the sky above a fixed point on the Earth's surface.

global divide: the divide with respect to access of information between different countries and different types of holders of information worldwide.

green IT: the practice of reducing energy consumption from IT equipment and thereby improving sustainability.

hacking: a method of gaining unauthorised access to a computer system/network.

hacker: someone who gains unauthorised access to a computer system/network.

hardware-assisted virtualisation: a guest OS is recompiled prior to installation inside a virtual machine allowing for an interface to the virtual machine that can differ from that of the underlying hardware.

honeypot: a server or computer system set up as a decoy to gather information on intruders or attackers of computer systems/networks.

hypervisor: hardware virtualisation technique enabling multiple operating systems to run on a single host system simultaneously.

information formats: the different ways in which information can be presented using www technologies, for example using social media or podcasts.

information styles: the style of the information regardless of whether technology is used or not, for example audio could be a recording of a podcast or someone giving a presentation.

Internet of Things: futuristic concept in which ordinary physical objects will be connected to the internet and be able to identify themselves to other devices.

input device: a hardware or peripheral device that allows a user to interact with a computer by sending data and instructions to it.

intrusion detection system (IDS): software that monitors computer system/network activities for unexpected or malicious activities.

link layer: the protocol layer that handles the moving of data in and out across a physical link in a network.

malware: software designed to cause disruption or damage to data and/or a computer system/network.

modem (cable): MODulator/DEModulator – a hardware device that enables a computer to send and receive information over telephone lines by converting digital data into an analogue signal.

modem (DSL): a hardware device that allows a computer to communicate with an ISP over a DSL connection; a traditional phone line (RJ-11) connects to the back of the DSL modem and the Cat5 (ethernet) cable connects the modem to a router or computer.

motherboard: a printed circuit board connecting all the peripherals and components of a computer, enabling them to communicate; it regulates the power received by the hard drive, graphics card, CPU and system memory from the power supply.

output device: a peripheral that receives data and instructions from a computer system to display, project or physically reproduce data that has been processed or stored.

paravirtualisation: architectural support facilitating the building of a virtual machine monitor that allows a guest OS to run in isolation.

penetration testing: a software tool that tests a computer system/network to identify vulnerabilities that could be exploited by an attacker.

processor: carries out the instructions of a computer program; it performs the mathematical, logical and input/output operations of a computer system.

real time: a level of computer responsiveness that a user senses as sufficiently immediate or that enables the computer to keep up with some external process.

resolution: the number of horizontal and vertical pixels on a monitor; the higher the number of pixels, the higher the resolution. More screen image can be displayed without scrolling. The image is sharper, but the icons and text will look smaller.

stakeholder: a person with an interest or concern in something, a person and/or a business.

virtualisation: creating logical resources from physical resources.